SENECA ON THE STAGE

MNEMOSYNE

BIBLIOTHECA CLASSICA BATAVA

COLLEGERUNT

A. D. LEEMAN · H. W. PLEKET · C. J. RUIJGH

BIBLIOTHECAE FASCICULOS EDENDOS CURAVIT

C. J. RUIJGH, KLASSIEK SEMINARIUM, OUDE TURFMARKT 129, AMSTERDAM

SUPPLEMENTUM NONAGESIMUM SEXTUM

DANA FERRIN SUTTON

SENECA ON THE STAGE

LUGDUNI BATAVORUM   E. J. BRILL   MCMLXXXVI

SENECA ON THE STAGE

BY

DANA FERRIN SUTTON

LEIDEN   E.J. BRILL   1986

ISBN 90 04 07928 9

PRINTED IN THE NETHERLANDS BY E. J. BRILL

CONTENTS

ACKNOWLEDGEMENTS

I should like to thank Professor William M. Calder III for reading an earlier draft of this study. We share the conviction that Seneca was writing for actual performance although, for reasons set forth below, we are sharply divided about the kind of performance for which Seneca's plays were meant. Nevertheless I have learned a lot from Professor Calder's critique and have been heartened by his encouragement. I must also record my thanks to Professors Gilbert Lawall and B.P. Reardon for providing me with various kinds of advice. First and foremost, I once again must express my gratitude to my wife, Dr. Kathryn A. Sinkovich, for her patience and encouragement as I wrote this study.

INTRODUCTION

One of the ways in which a dramatic work may be analysed is production criticism, according to which the text is regarded as a script intended for dramatic performance and one inquires how the playwright intended the play to be mounted on the stage. In the case of ancient drama the need for such examination is especially urgent because there are virtually no stage directions. Indications how the play is meant to be staged must be inferred from the text itself. Naturally, one brings to such analysis a knowledge of the dramatic resources available to the playwright and also the theatrical conventions prevalent in his time, insofar as such information can be gleaned from archaeology and antiquarian research.

With one exception, production criticism has been more or less systematically applied to the extant works of all the playwrights of antiquity, and such investigation constitutes a thriving branch of classical scholarship.[1] The exception, of course, is Senecan tragedy, because of a widespread (although by no means universal) conviction that the plays of the Senecan corpus were written to be read, or at most recited, but not to be produced on the stage.

This idea, which is unsupported by any ancient evidence, was first set forth by A.W. Schlegel in the first decade of the nineteenth century and has been maintained by some, but scarcely all, more recent authorities.[2] It is a view that, as originally put forward by Schlegel, is really an expression of taste: a reaction to the rhetorical and sometimes static nature of Senecan tragedy. Some subsequent authorities, most notably Otto

---

[1] Modern examples of this kind of work include C.W. Dearden's *The Stage of Aristophanes* (London, 1976) and Oliver Taplin's *The Stagecraft of Aeschylus* (Oxford, 1978).

[2] The idea that Seneca's plays were not meant for the stage was first advanced by A.W. Schlegel in *Vorlesungen über dramatische Kunst* (1809); cf. E. Lefevre, *Seneca's Tragödien* (Darmstadt, 1972) 13f. More recent authorities who have affirmed this view include J. Hippler, *Anneanae quaestiones scaenicae* (diss. Giessen, 1926), B. Marti, "Seneca's Tragedies: A New Interpretation," *TAPA* 76 (1945) 216-246, William Beare, *The Roman Stage*[3] (London, 1964) 234-246, Otto Zwierlein, *Die Rezitationsdramen Senecas mit einem kritisch-exegetischen Anhang* (Meisenheim am Glan, 1966), Elaine Fantham, *Seneca's Troades* (Princeton, 1982) 34-49 and Norman T. Pratt, *Senecan Drama* (Chapel Hill, 1983) 15-21. Upholding the contrary view are Léon Herrmann, "Les Tragédies de Sénèque étaient-elles Destinées au Théâtre?" *RBPh* 1924, 841-846 as well as *Le Théâtre de Sénèque* (Paris, 1924) 153-196, Moses Hadas, "The Roman Stamp of Seneca's Tragedies," *AJP* 60 (1939) 220-231, Margarete Bieber, "Wurden die Tragödien des Senecas im Rom ausgeführt?" *MDAI(R)* 60-61 (1953-54) 100-106, and William M. Calder III, "The Size of the Chorus in Seneca's *Agamemnon*," *CP* 70 (1975) 32-35 (also *op. cit.* p. 37 n. 59 below). Cf. also R.J. Tarrant, "Senecan Drama and its Antecedents," *HSCP* 82 (1978) 216-263. For further bibliography cf. Zwierlein, *ib.* Anm. 5 and 6.

Zwierlein,[3] have sought to buttress this contention by appeal to more concrete considerations. But this argument ignores important facts. In the first place, it is well known that Seneca's plays have been successfully performed in the Renaissance (which was scarcely bothered by Senecan rhetoric) and indeed in our own time.[4] In the second, in Seneca's plays we often see a striving after impressive and electrifying effects achieved by both verbal and (as implied by the text) visual means. This attempt to achieve genuine theatricality might well seem appropriate for *Bühnendrama* more than for *Lesedrama* or *Rezitationsdrama*.

But the most important consideration is that, if Seneca's tragedies were not written with actual performance in mind, their author at the very minimum maintains the fiction that they are destined for the stage. Nowadays playwrights employ stage directions or even more elaborate devices such as production books to indicate how they wish their plays to be performed, and such information, supplemental to the words written to be spoken by the actors, properly deserves to be regarded as an integral part of the "text" of the play. In the absence of such conventions,[5] the ancient playwrights were obliged to insert material into their texts that might be designated implicit stage directions: information about *mise-en-scène*, entrances and exits, stage business, etc.

Senecan tragedy contains textual information that looks very much like the sort of implicit stage directions one encounters in any other ancient plays: besides the kind of information just noted, for example, Seneca's texts seem to imply the availability of a stage building serving as the setting for each play and of the regular furniture of the classical theater. And, as already said, the texts imply that the generally static and rhetorical nature of Senecan tragedy is at least occasionally varied by stage business, sometimes of a quite impressive kind.

So the debate about Seneca and the stage really amounts to this: are these implicit stage directions meant to show how to produce these plays in the Roman theater and do they reflect any genuine solicitude for questions of dramaturgy on the part of the author? Are they coherent and

---

[3] Throughout this study Zwierlein will regularly be cited as an authority for the ideas against which I argue, being the most recent and usually the best exponent of the position he holds and subsuming previous discussions. It often happens that argumentation on some point has an extensive history, as indicated by Zwierlein.

[4] Senecan tragedies were of course performed in universities and schools in England during the reign of Henry VIII and Elizabeth: e.g. a performance of *Troades* at Trinity College, Cambridge, during the 1551-1552 year noted by J.W. Duff, *A Literary History of Rome in the Silver Age* (London, 1927) 271 (cf. also Fantham, *op. cit.* 49 n. 25). Ted Hughes' 1969 translation of the *Oedipus* has also been successfully performed.

[5] For some reason the few stage directions that do exist refer to sound effects, as at Aeschylus, *Eumenides* 120.

meaningful indications of what Seneca had in mind or only, as has in fact been maintained,[6] a polite fiction, an unimportant bow to literary convention? If we can answer these questions, we shall have gone as far as we can towards divining the poet's intentions.

At first sight, certain indications would seem to suggest that Seneca's implicit stage directions ought to be taken seriously. Consider, for example, a detail in the final act of the *Medea*. After the heroine kills one child at ground level, she goes into her house and ascends to the roof in order to kill the second and to mount her chariot, and the actor playing Medea is given only four lines to make this trip. But as Medea leaves the stage Iason orders his retainers to attack the house, and so it looks as if Seneca has borrowed a bit of stage business from his Euripidean model (Eur. *Me.* 1314ff.) and adapted it to a new purpose so as to give his actor time to make this ascent. Or again, new characters are usually identified in the text, but this is not always done. In the theater the absence of such identification cues need not be troublesome as long as we can reasonably assume that an audience could identify a new character by purely visual means. But in recitation the absence of verbal identification cues might prove vexing, as noted in greater detail below.

But such indications as these are scarcely probative. What is obviously required is a close examination that poses such questions as whether Seneca's implicit stage directions make dramaturgic sense and whether his plays could be produced in accordance with the resources and the conventions of the Roman theater. Such is our task.

However if we are to undertake such a study we must be sure to heed a couple of caveats. The first is that we should not automatically regard signs of Seneca's ineptitude as a dramatist as evidence that he was not writing for the stage. For a common tactic adopted by those arguing against Seneca as a stage poet is to demonstrate various compositional weaknesses and errors and to ask the reader to assume that such lapses tell against the idea that Seneca was writing for the stage, on the grounds that errors which might elude detection in reading or in recitation would become painfully and intolerably evident to an actual audience. But one may query this assumption. More likely the truth is the exact opposite: errors that would escape the notice of a theatergoer caught up in the excitement of a play would reveal themselves most clearly to the thoughtful and dispassionate reader, most especially if the reader in question is a scholar disposed to detect errors, inconsistencies, and illogicalities.

---

[6] So W.S. Barrett in his 1964 Oxford commentary on Euripides' *Hippolytus*, 16f.

A closely allied tactic is to compare the plays of Seneca to those of such poets as Aeschylus, Sophocles, Euripides, and Aristophanes, invariably to Seneca's discredit. Again, it is difficult to grasp the relevance of the large majority of such comparisons. In the first place, theatrical conventions prevalent in Seneca's day may have differed considerably from those of earlier times: as we shall see, for example, this is true of the onstage representation of bloodshed. In the second, whether Seneca was or was not writing for the stage, he was by the most favorable appraisal a gifted dilettante (although it should be remembered that various compositional errors have been demonstrated in the works of some of the playwrights with whom he is compared).[7] Therefore one wonders at the legitimacy of comparing his dramaturgy with that of professional playwrights and genuine men of the theater, and we may be led to wrong conclusions if we judge Senecan dramaturgy by inappropriate standards.

So our task is to examine Seneca's dramaturgy as indicated by the internal evidence of his plays. In the course of such a study one must naturally be vigilant for features that unambiguously disprove the contention that his plays were written for the stage or clearly establish their *Lesedrama* nature. In the absence of such evidence, there really are no grounds for doubting that these plays were written for production. The most that might reasonably be claimed is that some of the errors and inconsistencies which undeniably do exist in Senecan drama are signs that the plays in which they appear were not actually produced during Seneca's lifetime, or else they would have been put right in rehearsal. But this assertion scarcely reflects on their author's intention in writing them. Furthermore, many difficulties that have been alleged by previous students are not genuinely bothersome: a scholar bent on discovering problems is more likely to find them than to invent solutions. But if one approaches the study of Senecan tragedy with the assumption that these plays were meant for the stage, and so seeks to solve evident production problems, solutions often lie ready at hand.

Of course, evidence exists for the recitation of plays in antiquity, although the practice was not early or as widespread as has been claimed.[8]

---

[7] This is notably true of Aristophanes. Difficulties are found in such plays as the *Clouds* (compare 549ff. where Cleon is spoken of as dead with 586ff. where he is discussed as still living) and the *Plutus* (cf. H. Flashar, "Zur Eigenart des aristophanischen Spätwerks," in H.J. Newiger, *Aristophanes und die alte Komödie*, Darmstadt, 1975, 405ff.) One might also mention, for example, the compositional difficulties in Euripides' satyric *Cyclops* discussed by Peter D. Arnott, "The Overworked Playwright," *G&R* n. s. 8 (1961) 164-169.

[8] Evidence supposed to attest ancient plays meant for reading and recitation rather than for the stage is collected by Zwierlein, *op. cit.* 127-166. But in the first place the Greek evidence must be set aside. Cf. O. Crusius at *Festschr. Theodor Gomperz* (Vienna, 1902) 381-397, 54, Rudolf Pfeiffer, *History of Classical Scholarship to the End of the Hellenistic Age*

However it is not clear that such a thing as a *Rezitationsdrama*, in the sense of a play that (like, say, *Peer Gynt*) was written exclusively for reading or at most for recitation, ever existed.[9] Further, the problem must be faced that we have no sure idea how a play would have been recited:[10] by a single reciter "doing voices" or by several reciters? If the idea of Senecan tragedy as *Rezitationsdrama* serves to gloss over many problems, as its proponents suggest, it creates a major difficulty of its own. If the problem of identifying characters is significant in a stage play, it is far more pressing in recitation. In a stage play, you only have to identify a character (usually but not always by a verbal cue) on his first appearance. Thereafter the audience can be trusted to identify him by sight. In recitation, it would seem necessary to identify each character anew in every scene in which he appears. This of course is not done in Senecan tragedy. Therefore, to whoever claims that in some way Senecan tragedy shows signs of having not been seriously intended for the stage, we are able, among other things, to respond with the argument *tu quoque*: these plays do not show the signs of having *not* been written for the stage that one might expect to encounter. In view of the prevalent importance of *recitatio* in Seneca's time, it is by no means unlikely that certain passages such as extended monologues and descriptive passages (including passages describing concurrent stage business, a peculiarity of Senecan technique)[11] may have been written with recitation in mind. But it is quite possible that the writing of such hypothetical display-pieces was an interest subordinated to the composition of stage plays.

If Seneca's tragedies were not actually written for performance, the pretense that they were is maintained with remarkable industry and fidelity, and it should be incumbent on whoever wishes to argue that they were not meant for the stage to show why their author was intent on maintaining this fiction. Therefore the premise that these plays were intended for the stage will be adopted as a working hypothesis here, not to

---

(Oxford, 1968) 28f. and Howard Jacobson, "Two Studies on Ezechiel the Tragedian," *GRBS* 22 (1981) 168. See also the next note.

[9] When at *Rhetoric* 3.12 p. 1413 b 3ff. Aristotle writes of οἱ ἀναγνωστικοί, he may be speaking of something such as "dramatic poets especially worth reading" or "worth reading more than performing": cf. Crusius, *loc. cit.* and references given by Zwierlein, 129 n.l. According to C.J. Herington, *Cambridge History of Ancient Literature* 2.519, a remark of Quintilian (11.373) is significant, a reference to *iis quae ad scaenam componuntur fabulis*. But what are the alternatives to such *fabulae*? Plays written for reading? For recitation? As mere paper-exercises? Or could Quintilian use this phrase merely to distinguish the definition "plays" from the second definition of *fabulae*, "myths and stories"?

[10] This subject is ventilated by B. Walker in her review of Zwierlein's monograph at *CP* 64 (1969) 185. Cf. also Fantham, *op. cit.* 46-48.

[11] Cf. below p. 22 n. 27.

be abandoned unless proven untenable, and Seneca's tragedies will be subjected to systematic production criticism. In Part I we shall consider his use of the physical and human resources of the theater, and in Part II we shall examine those passages that appear to be implicit stage directions, or more precisely the four most important kinds of stage direction, entrance cues, exit cues, cues that identify new characters, and indications of stage business. Ample evidence will emerge to document the claims made in this Introduction: nothing in Senecan tragedy could not have been produced on the ancient stage, and in their use of striking stage effects (as well, of course, as in other ways that lie beyond the scope of this study) these plays exhibit a theatricality and also, as it seems, a striving after popular appeal thoroughly redolent of the stage.

This study is primarily devoted to the corpus of plays that are complete and authentic: the *Hercules Furens, Troades, Medea, Phaedra, Oedipus, Agamemno*, and *Thyestes*, abbreviated respectively as *H. F., Tr., Me., Ph., Oed., Ag.*, and *Th.* and normally discussed in this order without prejudice about any special significance in this ordering. Also found in the Senecan corpus are one incomplete tragedy (if all the sketches collected under this title in fact pertain to a single play), the *Phoenissae (Phoen.)*, and two inauthentic ones, the *Hercules Oetaeus (H. Oet.)* and the *Octavia.*[12] The *Octavia* is ignored here altogether since I have studied its dramaturgy elsewhere. However, after some hesitation I have decided to take into account the *Hercules Oetaeus* and *Phoenissae*. Although the *Hercules Oetaeus* is entirely inauthentic—indeed, this study brings to light a couple of ways in which its dramaturgy differs from that of genuine Senecan tragedy—the play retains a certain interest since the possibility exists that its author imitated Seneca's dramatic technique as well as other features of his style, and in any event it attests theatrical conditions of approximately Seneca's time. The *Phoenissae* sketches might also present features of interest.

---

[12] For the *Herucules Oetaeus* cf. W.-H. Friedrich, "Sprach unf Stil des *Hercules Oetaeus*," *Hermes* 82 (1954) 51-84 and B. Axelson, *Korruptelenkult: Studien zur Textkritik der unechten Seneca—Tragödie Hercules Oetaeus* (Lund, 1967). To be sure, some think that the play may contain some authentic Senecan material (cf. Michael Coffey at *Lustrum* 2, 1957, 141f.). But what material might that be? At first sight the *Octavia* looks inauthentic because it "predicts" events that transpired after the death of Seneca: the revolt of Vindex and the killing of Nero. This impression is confirmed by the un-Senecan nature of both the language and the internal economy of the play: cf. R. Helm, *Die Praetexta "Octavia"* at *SB-Berlin* 1934, 283-347 and D.F. Sutton, *The Dramaturgy of the Octavia* (Königstein/Taunus, 1983).

PART ONE

USE OF THE THEATER AND ITS RESOURCES

I. USE OF DRAMATIC SPACE AND THE *SCAENAE FRONS*

Drama requires the creation of a fictitious space clearly distinct from the real space inhabited by the audience. The initial creation of such dramatic space is not entirely the playwright's responsibility since it is demarcated by the very architecture of the theater. However a playwright must give dramatic space a specific identity for the purpose of his play and also, so to speak, impose a structure on this space. That is to say, he must create a setting and, at least in the case of some plays, establish relationships between the visible locality of the stage-set and other localities that are offstage and therefore invisible. In the case of an ancient drama, the physical setting is usually created by giving a fictitious identity to the stage building (as the royal palace of Corinth, Philoctetes' cave, or whatever might be required). If it is necessary to relate the locality of the stage setting to other, offstage, localities, this is done by indicating that a given avenue of exit leads to some stated place.

In order to orient the audience, it is necessary to convey information about the way the fictitious space of the stage is organized. To some extent this information might be supplied visually, but the playwright primarily announces his *mise-en-scène* by placing orienting information in his text. Normally such information is provided at or at least near the beginning of the play. An effective and efficient way of doing this is found in the prologue of Menander's *Dyscolus*. The audience is explicitly told (tr. Lionel Casson):

> I want you to imagine that this (*with a sweeping gesture*) is Phyle, near Athens, and that this cave I've just come out of is the famous sanctuary of the nymphs that belongs to the people of Phyle and the others who manage to coax crops out of the stones around here. Now, the property on my right here belongs to Cnemon...When the situation got as bad as it could possibly be and her life was nothing but bitterness and hardship, his wife left him and went to live with the son she had had by her former husband. He has a scrap of land (*pointing*) adjoining here and he barely manages to squeeze enough from it to feed himself, his mother, and single faithful old servant...

Once this structure is imposed on the fictitious space of the stage, the entrances and exits of the actors must be engineered so as to match. The door of the *scaenae frons* is the entrance to the sanctuary, the "stage right" side entrance leads to Cnemon's farm, and the "stage left" side entrance leads to the farm occupied by the ex-wife and son. An actor who exits to "Cnemon's farm" must depart by the proper side entrance, and when he returns to the stage he must come back by the same way. Now, of course, in many plays the fictitious purpose of the side entrances is not named, but presumably an actor who exits by a particular route should reenter by the same way. Only in these cases the specific comings and goings of the actors cannot be reconstructed from the text.

In ancient drama the particulars of the stage setting are not always enunciated so baldly, but it is usual to provide information of this order towards the beginning of the play. Not so in Seneca. Adequate information about the stage setting is given in his plays, but in some of them such information tends to "leak out" over the course of the entire play rather than being supplied at the beginning.

In the *Hercules Furens* the first such spatial information we are given is simply that Iuno is on earth, deserting the heavens whence she has been "banished by concubines" (3f.). At 134f. we are first informed that the setting is at Thebes:

> *iam Cadmeis incluta Bacchis*
> *aspersa die dumeta rubent*

Not until 506ff. are we told that the *scaenae frons* represents a temple, when Lycus bids his attendants:

> *congerite silvas; templa supplicibus suis*
> *iniecta flagrent, coniugem et totum gregem*
> *consumat unus igne subiecto rogus.*

The stage building plays an important part during the killing of the children. The deluded hero imagines that the temple is Lycus' palace and that his sons who have taken refuge within it are hiding in the royal house (999ff.):

> *huc eat et illuc valva deiecto obice*
> *rumpatque postes; culmen impulsem labet.*
> *perlucet omnis regia; hic video abditum*
> *natum scelesti patris.*

An alleged problem exists.[1] Hercules kills Megara and one son inside the stage building, yet in Act V the corpses of Megara and both sons are visible onstage. But it suffices to suggest that at some point, probably at the beginning of that act, the bodies are brought onstage by extras. There is good precedent for this assumption in Aeschylus' *Agamemnon*. Both Agamemnon and Cassandra are killed offstage, in the palace. The corp-

---

[1] Zwierlein, *op. cit.* 42f.

ses are brought onstage in time for Clytaemnestra to gloat over them in her speech at 1372ff. although the text gives no indication how they are transported onto the stage.[2] So the appearance of the corpses in the *Hercules Furens* betokens no confusion or contradiction regarding the setting of the play.

In the *Troades* the first information supplied the audience is that the smoking ruins of Troy are visible to Hecuba in the prologue. The actor delivering these lines must be looking off ''into the wings'' and in so doing establishes the direction of the city. Not until 483ff. are we told that the scene is set before the tomb of Hector, when Andromacha says:

> *est tumulus ingens coniugis cari sacer,*
> *verendus hosti, mole quem immensa parens*
> *opibusque magnis struxit*

Later we are supplied a bit more specific information about the appearance of this tomb when Ulixes threatens (664f.):

> *pergam et e summo aggere*
> *traham sepulchra.*

This is only one of a number of tombs that dot the Trojan landscape—surely a symbolic touch—as we are told at 893ff. And of course the offstage tomb of Achilles figures prominently in the play as the venue of Polyxena's sacrifice (cf. especially 1121ff.). No information is provided about the physical relationship of these two tombs save that the tomb of Achilles is visible to one standing atop that of Hector (1086f.). But it might be a reasonable surmise that, if by looking up one side entrance Hecuba establishes that such is the direction of Troy, the other side entrance leads to Achilles' tomb.

The allegation has been made that there are at least two textually unmarked changes of scene in the *Troades*.[3] After Talthybius addresses the captive Trojan women in their camp, he exits abruptly. Agamemno and Pyrrhus appear conversing. The reason for their presence is unexplained. They know about the earth tremor and the apparition of Achilles' ghost, facts about which the captive women need to be informed in the first part

---

[2] To be sure, it is not quite clear how the corpses are produced in the *Agamemnon* (and for that matter also the *Choephoroi*). The simplest way would be to have them produced by extras, maybe unceremoniously thrown out the palace door. However the suggestion has been made by John Gould at *The Cambridge History of Classical Literature* 1.270 that in both plays the corpses were produced on the *eccyclema*. But where is there evidence for the availability of the *eccyclema* in the Aeschylean theater? Nonetheless, especially if Gould is right, the possibility may exist that the corpses in the *Hercules Furens* were produced on the *eccyclema*-like *exostra*. But in both Aeschylus and Seneca the use of extras for this purpose seems simpler and more probable.

[3] Zwierlein, *ib.* 39f., Fantham *op. cit.* 37-39.

of Act II; and the subject of their discussion with Calchas, the need to kill
Polyxena and Astyanax, should not be overheard by the chorus (especially as the news that Polyxena is to be sacrificed comes as a shock to
Hecuba and the Trojan women in Act IV). Then there must be a second
textually unadvertised shift of scene, as the setting of Act III is again the
camp of the Trojan captives.

According to Fantham there is another change of scene in Act IV. In
the first place, this is supposed to be signalled by 930ff.:

> num per has vastum in mare
> volvenda rupes, latere quas scisso levat
> altum vadoso Sigeon spectans sinu?

For *has rupes* suggests that the scene has shifted to Sigeum. Furthermore,
mention of warriors' tombs lying scattered across the Trojan plain at
893-895 is taken as an indication that Achilles' tomb is visible onstage
(although this involves yet another shift of scene, since Achilles' tomb
would scarcely be visible in Act V, when Polyxena's sacrifice is
narrated).

If such analyses of the settings of the *Troades* were correct, then the
charge could appropriately be laid that the play displays an uncertain
sense of place such as one would scarcely expect to encounter in a stage
drama,[4] especially since none of these shifts of scene is explicitly indicated.[5] But this whole tissue of suppositions about the setting of the
Troades is misguided.

In the first place, to dispose of alleged changes of scene in Acts IV and
V, the deictic *has* at line 930 is a weak peg from which to hang a conse-
quential argument. Surely this pronoun need not mean that the cliffs of
Sigeum are immediately present. Probably this pronoun is simply to be
accompanied by a gesture as the actor playing Hecuba points in the appropriate direction, and if in Greek tragedy a demonstrative pronoun
often indicates nothing more specific than a person or thing present in the
speaker's mind, the same may well be true in a Latin one. Furthermore,
it seems intrinsically wrongheaded to haul down a copy of Strabo, as does
Fantham, in order to document the fact that the cliffs of Sigeum were
situated at a considerable remove from the Trojan shore. Probably no an-

---

[4] Although if we were to imitate Zwierlein and bring Aristophanes as well as the Greek
tragedians into discussion, even this verdict would appear less firmly warranted. Consider
the *Acharnians*. This play contains various settings, such as the Pnyx, the house of
Euripides, and somewhere in the countryside where Dicaeopolis sets up his trading sta-
tion. The transitions between these settings are not clearly marked and are left to the
reader's inference.

[5] As will be shown in connection with the *Hercules Oetaeus*, it would seem that in ancient
tragedy the normal way to indicate a change of scene was to withdraw the chorus from the
stage and have it reenter at the new location.

cient play could withstand such rationalistic criticism. And it is hard to see how the idea that Achilles' tomb is at any point visible to the audience can be extracted from the statement at 893ff.

The idea that there is a scene-shift during Act II of the *Troades* (and such a change of setting seems especially improbable in mid-act) also results from the subjection of an ancient tragedy to an overly rationalistic criticism that ignores the artificial conventions of the theater. Although the location of the interview between Agamemno and Pyrrhus in the camp of the Trojan women may defy logic, one must remember that a theatrical tradition that in the main eschewed changes of scene within plays would perforce be tolerant of scenes such as the present one that, properly speaking, should be staged elsewhere.[6] Another convention of the ancient theater was that once the chorus enters in the parodos, it remains onstage until the end of the play. This convention entails the artificial and somewhat illogical presence of the chorus in all kinds of scenes at which by any rational account they should not be present, sometimes because they overhear information they should not receive. And, in such cases, if they were to transmit such information to other characters so as to disrupt the flow of the action, this is not done.[7] Such is the artificial convention of the Greek tragic stage and we cannot hold Seneca to more stringent standards. Alternatively, if you demand a more rational accounting of the present scene, it might have been possible to stage the interview of Agamemno, Pyrrhus, and Calchas so as it was not overheard by the chorus. After all, there are points in Senecan drama at which a character says something not overheard by another (asides, and even more extended speeches in a dramatic technique developed from the aside).[8]

The *Medea*, as Zwierlein observed,[9] requires a two-building "set". That the palace fronts the stage is shown by 177f.:

> sed cuius ictu regius cardo strepit?
> ipse est Pelasgo tumidus imperio Creo.

Creon enters from the palace, while Medea and the Nutrix stand in front of Medea's house. He speaks a non-overheard monologue, and then Medea crosses to his part of the stage (186).

---

[6] The sacrifice scene in the *Medea* is another scene to which this statement applies.

[7] According to Tarrant, *op. cit.* 224 this is a peculiarity of Seneca. But in fact this dramatic convention has Greek precedents. Cf. Roy C. Flickinger, *The Greek Theater and its Drama*[4] (Chicago, 1936) 150-161 (especially 156f.). Cf. further below, pp. 39-41. It ought to be added that the idea that Senecan choruses are routinely withdrawn during acted episodes is demonstrably wrong, as will be shown below.

[8] See below, p. 39.

[9] *Op. cit.* 40f.

That Medea's house fronts the stage is suggested by the consideration that it would be very unreasonable to have a divorced Medea still living in the palace. Better to have her living in her own house, as in Euripides. And at 973f. she announces she is going to climb to the roof:

> *excelsa nostrae tecta conscendam domus*
> *caede inchoata.*

Then too, if the play were set only in front of the palace, it might seem illogical for her to offer her sacrifice to Hecate and prepare her poisons in full view of her enemies. This objection is at least mitigated if she conducts this sacrifice before her own house: the fictitious space between the two buildings could, by artificial dramatic convention, be understood as greater than the actual stage-space.

Finally, at 995ff. the Nuntius describes the burning of the palace. Later, when Medea appears on the roof of her house, Iason bids his followers (995ff.):

> *en ipsa tecti parte praecipiti imminet.*
> *huc rapiat ignes aliquis, ut flammis cadat*
> *suis perusta.*

It would be nonsense for Iason to command the burning of a building already consumed by fire. He is ordering one of his followers to transfer fire from the smouldering ruin of the palace to Medea's house.

That the stage building in the *Phaedra* represents the royal palace at Athens is first established by line 384:

> *sed en, patescunt regiae fastigia.*

Furthermore, at 82ff. it is indicated that one of the side entrances leads to Hippolytus' beloved forest:

> *vocor in silvas.*
> *hac, hac pergam qua via longum*
> *compensat iter.*

At line 580 Phaedra enters, faints, then plays out her scene with Hippolytus. When he leaves, the Nutrix raises the alarm that Hippolytus was trying to rape Phaedra and summons the palace slaves. Then at line 733 she gives the order *proferte in urbem.* If this command means "carry Phaedra to the city" it is puzzling: why take her to the city when the palace is comfortably at hand? Worse yet, Phaedra is next heard of uttering a terrible cry within the palace (850ff.) so that Seneca is seemingly guilty of having a character exit in one direction but reenter from another.

Perceiving this problem, Léon Herrmann wished to emend the text to *proferte in aedes*. But a better suggestion has been made.[10] The Nutrix has just been loudly accusing Hippolytus of attempted rape and *proferte in urbem* means "carry news of this disaster to the city." Then Phaedra is picked up and carried into the palace, as is only natural. To be sure, this solution deprives this scene of an exit cue for Phaedra, but in view of the large number of uncued exits in Senecan tragedy (a subject to which we shall eventually return) this is not disturbing.

In the *Oedipus* we are told at line 202 that the stage building represents the royal house at Thebes:

> *quisnam ille propero regiam gressu petit?*

The *Agamemno* is the first play in which the setting is established in the prologue, when the Umbra Thyestis says (6f.):

> *video paternos, immo fraternos lares.*
> *hoc est vetustum Pelopiae limen domus*

The setting of the *Thyestes* looks intensely problematic. At the beginning of the play the Furia repeatedly urges the Tantali Umbra to visit the royal *domus* (23f., 33, 54f., 83ff., 100). Normally this information would suffice to establish that the *scaenae frons* represents the palace at Argos. Then too, Atreus' description of the physical upheaval of the palace at 260ff. seems to be a relation of what he sees, or thinks he sees, as he stands onstage.[11] But at 641ff. the Nuntius' speech begins:

> *in arce summa Pelopiae pars est domus*
> *conversa ad austros, cuius extremum latus*
> *aequale monti crescit atque urbem premit*

This is the way a tragic messenger speech describes some offstage locale. And at 901f. Atreus bids his slaves:

> *turba famularis, fores*
> *templi relaxa, festa patefiat domus.*

So, evidently, only at this late point in the play are we informed that the setting is in front of some temple where the ghastly banquet is held. But why hold a feast in a temple?

All of this seems desperately muddled and one can readily sympathize with Frank Justus Miller, the Loeb translator, who wrote "the scene is laid partly without the city of Argos, and partly within the royal palace," although he was unable to specify where this alleged shift of scene occurs.

---

[10] By Pierre Grimal in his *Erasme* edition of the play (Paris, 1965) in a note *ad loc*.

[11] Possibly imitating Naevius' *Lycurgus* (cf. frr. 48 and 52 Ribbeck[2]). For this scene cf. below p. 24.

Further problems can be noted. The setting ought to be before the palace for a variety of reasons. The *domus* of Pelops is constantly mentioned in the text and obviously has symbolic value: the Furia is trying to overturn the House of Pelops in both the literal and the figurative sense, and setting the play in front of the *domus regia* would give visual reinforcement to this verbal image. Then again, making the stage building the *domus* would allow for maximum use of the stage door as an entryway; otherwise, would it not have to be ignored for most of the play? And in line 902, why is the temple called a *festa domus*?

A first step towards making sense out of this seeming hash is to emend line 902 to read *fores / tecti relaxa* so as to eliminate the vexatious temple. The outstanding problem then remains the Nuntius' description of the palace. There is no reason for thinking that the *domus* of Atreus is a separate building from the palace of Pelops. Therefore the proper solution is to note that the Nuntius stresses that he is describing the south part of a building stated to be a huge structure. He is simply describing another part of the palace that does not happen to face the stage. We may rest assured that the *scaenae frons* does indeed represent the royal palace.

The *Hercules Oetaeus* features a change of scene, an uncommon although by no means unattested device in ancient tragedy.[12] The setting of the prologue is established by lines 101ff.:

> *vos pecus rapite ocius*
> *qua templa tollens acta Cenaei Iovis*
> *austro timendum spectat Euboicum mare.*

So the setting is now in Euboea. Unless the *scaenae frons* is supposed to represent the temple of Jupiter mentioned here, which seems an unnecessary conclusion, it is ignored for this act. The chorus of Iole's captive companions enters at line 104, but is withdrawn at 232, which seems to have been the traditional way of signalling a change of scene in classical tragedy.[13] During the first act we are prepared for the forthcoming change of location (cf. 135 *ad Trachina vocor* and 194f. *formam lacrimis aptate meis / resonetque malis aspera Trachin*). Thus at the beginning of Act II *Herculea coniunx* at line 241 establishes Deianira as the character who enters at 256 and 254 *sonuere postes* suffices to identify the *scaenae frons* as the protagonist's palace at Trachin.

---

[12] The classic example of a scene-change is of course Aeschylus' *Eumenides*. On the showing of *P. Oxy.* 20.2257 fr. 1 a shift of scene also occurred in Sophocles' satyric *Achilleos Erastae*, possibly in the same poet's *Troilus* (the papyrus was so interpreted by its editor, Edgar Lobel), and in Aeschylus' *Aetnae* (the real one or at least the spurious) there were no less then five such shifts.

[13] Or so it is commonly supposed by commentators on the *Eumenides*. While the text does not make it entirely clear that the chorus retires at 231 and reenters at 245, such appears a highly likely assumption.

At 194f. Iole laments:

> *formam lacrimis aptate meis*
> *resonetque malis aspere Trachin.*

Therefore according to Zwierlein[14] time takes an irrational jump forward and the shift from Euboea to Trachin occurs during Act I rather than at its end. But this idea is difficult to swallow.

Iole and the chorus know their destination (cf. 135 *ad Trachina vocor*) so that *resonet... Trachin* has at most a proleptic force. However it is tempting to interpret *resonet* not as a present subjunctive of *resono -are* but rather as a future indicative of a collateral third conjugation verb found in Ennius, Accius, and Pacuvius.

The first preserved scene of the *Phoenissae* is shown to be some barren spot, probably outside Thebes, by line 27, *est alius noster in silvis locus.* 358f. show that the setting of the next scene is the same:

> *nemo me ex his eruat*
> *silvis; latebo rupis exesae cavo*

So possibly the *scaenae frons* represents a cave mouth.[15] The setting of the remainder of the scenes attributed to the *Phoenissae* seems more problematic. In the scene commencing at 363 Antigone urges her mother Iocasta to interpose between the warring armies of her sons (403ff.). Obviously Antigone and the Nuntius are standing where they can see the contending forces. Then in another sketchy scene that seems to begin at line 443 Iocasta mediates between Polynices and Eteocles. Some think that these scenes involve at least one shift of locale, to the battlefield (although a battlefield would be a very unusual setting for a classical tragedy).[16] In the preceding scene are Antigone and Iocasta still in the woods or do they stand on city battlements and survey the scene in a *teichoscopia*? The easiest way of staging all of this material would be in imitation of Sophocles' *Oedipus Coloneus*, by locating the entire play in the original woodland setting and bringing Polynices and Eteocles to their mother rather than *vice versa*. Indeed, such may have been Seneca's actual intention, imperfectly expressed. Perhaps something was to intervene between the last two scenes, so that Iocasta reentered accompanied by her two sons. In any event, it is not absolutely clear that one, let alone two, changes of scene are implied by these *disjecta membra* of a tragedy, if

---

[14] *Op. cit.* 37f.

[15] For this setting cf. W. Jobst, *Die Höhle in griechischen Theater des 5. und 4. Jahrhunderte vor Christ* (Vienna, 1970).

[16] So F.J. Miller in his Loeb translation.

indeed all these sketches represent a single play.[17] Perhaps the proper conclusion is that Seneca wrote his plays by first sketching out the major scenes and by worrying about problems of stagecraft (and also writing connecting passages and choruses) at a later stage of composition.

II. Scenic Features

A. *The Stage Door*

In several of Seneca's tragedies attention is drawn to the door of the *scaenae frons*. As some character enters from the building someone else remarks on the creaking of the door on its hinges or on its opening: *Me.* 177, *Ph.* 384, *Oed.* 911 and 995, and also *H. Oet.* 254f. The audience's attention is directed to the door in other ways, as when Hercules seeks to tear down the doors of the temple in order to kill his children (*H. F.* 999ff.), when the door of the tomb is barred to protect Astyanax (*Tr.* 512), when Theseus orders the door be opened and pulls out Phaedra in order to confront her (*Ph.* 863) and also when he orders the palace door be opened at the end of the play (1275), when the Furia bids the palace door be decorated with laurel (*Th.* 54), and when the door is opened later in the play to discover an interior scene.

Since the *Medea* uses a two-building "set," in this play alone the side doors of the *scaenae frons* (the *hospitalia* of Vitruvius 5.6.8) are used.

B. *The Interior of the Stage Building*

Besides the visible space before the *scaenae frons* and the fictitious off-stage spaces mentioned in the text and sometimes accessed by the side entrances, another fictitious space is the interior of the structure represented by the stage building. Sometimes important action can occur here. At *Hercules Furens* 1002ff. Amphitryo stands at the stage door and describes to the audience the killing of the children and Megara. The verisimilitude of this staging is enhanced by the cries of Hercules and

---

[17] As an alternative to the idea that the *Phoenissae* sketches are the remains of a play never completed by its author, some have proposed that they are the remains of a complete play severely mangled in mss. transmission. But certain facts brought to light in the present study tell against this latter idea. We have just seen that the setting of the play does not seem well thought out. Later we shall also see that these sketches are remarkably devoid of passages that invite interpretation as implicit stage directions (this is especially true of verbal cues that identify new characters for the audience). Hence it is tempting to think that these sketches look the way they do because Seneca had not yet turned his attention to production problems.

Megara issuing from within.[18] In the *Medea* it is at least once, maybe twice, supposed that the actor representing Medea can move between the *pulpitum* and the roof by travelling within that building. But in other plays the interior of the stage building is represented visibly, as noted below.

C. *The Roof of the Stage Building*

In the *Hercules Furens* Iuno presumably appears on the *theologeion* and in the *Medea* the protagonist kills one son and takes the other and heads for the roof (973f.):

> excelsa nostrae tecta conscendam domus
> caede inchoata.

The top of the stage building may also be used in an earlier scene of the same play. At 380f. the Nutrix asks:

> alumna, celerem quo rapis tectis pedem?
> persiste et iras comprime ac retine impetum.

In the absence of a preposition it is unclear what is meant by *tectis*: does Medea come out of the stage building or is she atop it?

This same ambiguity occurs in the final act of the *Phaedra*. At 1154f. the chorus asks:

> quae vox ab altis flebilis tectis sonat
> strictoque vaecors Phaedra quid ferro parat?

This scene is deemed problematic.[19] For Theseus sees Phaedra and asks (1156ff.):

> quis te dolore percitam instigat furor?
> quid ensis iste quidve vociferatio
> planctusque supra corpus invisum volunt?

Thereupon Phaedra launches into a monologue in which she addresses Theseus (1164f.) and also the corpse of Hippolytus (1168ff.). At the end of this speech she casts herself on the sword and dies.

The supposed difficulty is that the chorus seems to locate Phaedra on the roof of the palace, but then she addresses Theseus and the dead Hippolytus as if she were on the *pulpitum*. One could of course challenge the assumption that *ab altis...tectis* ought to be interpreted "from the high

---

[18] Nothing similar, of course, occurs in Euripides' *Heracles*. But the way the killing of the Niobids was probably staged in Sophocles' *Niobe* (Artemis and Apollo standing at the palace door, shooting at the girls within, with shrieks emanating from the palace) presents a distinct precedent.

[19] Zwierlein, *op. cit.* 13-18.

roof'' rather than "from the lofty building," as the latter interpretation would obviate the objection. Nevertheless there may be reason for preferring to locate Phaedra on the roof: this assumption would explain why nobody seeks to interfere with her suicide. But in any event the assumption that Phaedra is on the roof is only problematic to someone who cannot accept that a person standing on a roof can speak with people on ground level or recognize the identity of a corpse from such a distance.[20] No matter how one chooses to interpret the staging of the final act of the *Phaedra*, it is difficult to perceive any material problems here.

D. *Interior Scenes*

Two of the tragedies require some means of representing interior scenes. In the *Phaedra* the heroine is produced lying prostrate on her couch (384ff.):

> *sed en, patescunt regiae fastigia.*
> *reclinis ipsa sedis auratae toro*
> *solitos amictus mente non sana abnuit.*

On the basis of line 384 the suggestion has been made that this scene was represented on the *fastigium*, the second storey of the stage building.[21] Presumably a curtain was drawn to reveal this scene and then drawn again at line 404 or soon thereafter. Thus the actor playing Phaedra could descend in order to reappear on the *pulpitum* at line 583.

No internal evidence speaks against this idea and if we were to think the scene to have been staged differently it might be hard to find a genuinely satisfying translation for *patescunt regiae fastigia*. But it is difficult to accept that the interior scene in the *Thyestes* was staged in this way. At lines 901f. (already quoted) Atreus bids his servants open the door to the palace. Thyestes is discovered within, having just completed his ghastly banquet. One assumes that Atreus' retainers accompany him at *pulpitum* level, and the natural way to stage this scene would be to have the extras throw open the door to the stage building and for the *exostra* to be produced. This was the item of machinery used to represent interiors in the Roman theater, mentioned by Cicero, *Prov. Cons.* 14 (for its Greek equivalent cf. particularly Pollux, *Onomasticon* 4.127 and 4.129): a device the same as or similar to the *eccyclema* of the classical Greek theater, a platform wheeled out the door to represent interiors.

---

[20] Further alleged problems concerning this corpse will be considered in a later context.

[21] So Grimal in a note *ad loc.* in his edition. This solution and its alternative, that the *exostra* was used, both imply the irrational consequence that the Nutrix and the chorus can see and overhear Phaedra's lament. But here is another example of the tolerated irrationality of theatrical convention.

E. *The Altar*

No scenic device is used in Senecan tragedy with more frequency than an altar, and for some reason our poet has a marked predilection for scenes involving sacrifice, both acted and described.[22]

In the *Hercules Furens* Amphitryo and his family take refuge at the altar in order to avoid Lycus' cruelty, and the king threatens to burn down the temple (503ff.). Later in the play the chorus of merrymakers that arrives to celebrate Hercules' victory addresses a sacrificial priest standing by the altar (893f.). Immediately thereafter the hero himself enters in order to offer a thanksgiving sacrifice to the gods. At 908ff. he bids his attendants prepare the sacrifice, but this gesture of piety is interrupted by the onset of his madness. After he has killed his children, Amphitryo stands at the altar and bids Hercules kill him as a last sacrifice (1039ff.). Thus the joyous sacrifice of hecatombs has been replaced by the slaughter of the hero's family at the altar and temple.

In the *Medea* there is a long passage (740ff.) in which Medea offers sacrifices to Hecate. From 807f. *manet noster / sanguis ad ara* it is evident that this scene is played at the stage altar, which seems to be specially gotten up to represent an appropriate place for chthonic sacrifice (797f.):

> *tibi sanguineo caespite sacrum*
> *solemne damus*

In the *Phaedra* the Nutrix states that Hippolytus is coming to perform sacrifice (424f.) and on the basis of this remark we might be tempted to guess that the stage setting contains an altar. This surmise is confirmed by 707ff.:

> *en impudicum crine contorto caput*
> *laeva reflexi, iustior numquam focis*
> *datus tuis est sanguis, arquitenens dea.*

Hippolytus strives to kill Phaedra at the altar, a sacrifice to his divine patroness.

The altar figures prominently in the *Oedipus*. At the beginning of the play, Oedipus stands at the altar, a suppliant to the gods, begging that his land be spared. Likewise the prostrate people come to the altars, asking for the release of death (197f.). Later comes one of the most remarkable scenes in ancient drama, which we shall have to consider in detail in a later context, when a bull and heifer are sacrificed at the stage altar.

---

[22] For altars in the public Roman theater cf. Donatus, *de Comoedia* 8.3. Wessner, *in scaenae duae arae poni solebant, dextra Liberi, sinistra eius dei, cui ludi fiebant.* Of course the tradition of the theatrical altar goes back to the Greek *thymele*.

In the *Agamemno* Eurybates stands at the altar as he gives thanks to the gods for his safe homecoming (392a ff.), and there is a somewhat sketchy gesture of thanksgiving as Agamemno and Clytemnestra stand at the altar (792). Later Electra takes refuge at the altar to avoid Clytemnestra's wrath (951).

These onstage scenes do not exhaust Seneca's enthusiasm for sacrificial scenes. We must also recall the sacrifice of Polyxena at the tomb of Achilles narrated in the *Troades* (1118ff.) and the fact that Atreus' murder of the children is described as a ghastly sacrifice in the *Thyestes* (641ff.).

F. *The Trap Door*

Two plays, the *Agamemno* and the *Thyestes*, begin with the appearance of a ghost. In the Roman theater the normal way to stage such apparitions was by the use of a trap door. The Bobbio Scholiast on Cicero, *pro Sestio* 126, helps us visualize how this would have been enacted, as he says that in Pacuvius' *Iliona* the Umbra Deiphobi appeared *ab inferiore aulaei parte*, which has been interpreted to mean "from a trap-door downstage, near, or part of, the groove into which the curtain sank."[23] When at *Ag.* 2 the Thyestis Umbra says *adsum profundo Tartari emissus specu*, these words may indicate that the actor is emerging from this trap door. No useful information is given in the text of the *Thyestes* about the staging of that apparition.

G. *Other Possible Features*

Such physical resources can be deduced from the texts of Senecan drama with assurance. Other resources are not so clearly attested but would have been useful and may have been employed.

The final departure of Medea at the end of the *Medea*, on the magic chariot, may have used the machine.

As we shall see, when some Senecan characters enter for the first time, their identity is not verbally established, and so one must assume that in such cases identification took place visually. By the same logic, if the physical settings of Senecan tragedies are not always textually established at the beginning of the play, we must remember that the use of painted scenery may have compensated for such absence of verbal information. Then too, the revolving scenic *periactoi* mentioned by Vitruvius 5.6.8 would have been useful for representing the change of scene in the *Her-*

---

[23] F.H. Wright, *Cicero and the Theater* (Northampton, Mass., 1931) 58 n. 61.

cules Oetaeus. The absence of the concluding choral *Schlusswort* might be explicable by reference to the curtain employed in the Roman theater, raised from a downstage trench at the end of the play.[24]

III. Scenic Effects

Seneca's tragedies are written so as to produce powerful effects on his audiences: thus his taste for rhetorical fireworks, the supernatural, and gore.[25] The texts of his plays repeatedly imply a similar striving for strong dramatic impact on the visual level. Some of the scenic effects in Senecan tragedy will be described more closely in connection with a discussion of implicit stage directions in Part II. For the moment it will suffice to notice the most outstanding such bits of business.

In the *Hercules Furens* visual effects come to the fore when the hero goes mad and kills his children. First he shoots down one son with his bow (991ff.). Then he launches a violent assault on the stage building, bursts down the door, and goes in after the remainder of his family. This scene represents an outburst of physical violence unprecedented, as far as we know, on the tragic stage.

Another visual effect in this play occurs in connection with the protagonist's first entrance. From 603 *hoc nefas* it would seem as if the infernal dog Cerberus is somehow produced onstage.

If the *Hercules Furens* is one play in which Seneca has altered a Euripidean model by adding more physical movement and violence, the *Medea* is another. Besides the appearance of the winged chariot, inherited from Euripides, this play features the onstage killing of the sons, the sacrifice in which the heroine slashes herself and drips blood over the altar (807ff.), the soldiers' frantic rush against Medea's house; it is also possible that the description of the burning palace was accompanied by some visual effects. And in Act V, as Medea stands atop her house, Iason bids his retainers set it afire (986).[26] Since the command to the extras to prepare a sacrifice in the *Hercules Furens* is not carried out, at least to completion, and since Ulixes' order to demolish the tomb is not executed in the *Troades*, we cannot be certain that Iason's order is obeyed here. But it may be possible that something was done to represent the house as burning as Medea makes her airborne escape.

---

[24] It has already been pointed out that a separate curtain would be required for the second-storey *fastigium* used to represent interior scenes.

[25] For the supernatural cf. Mary V. Braginton, *The Supernatural in Seneca's Tragedies* (diss. Yale, 1933) and for the gore cf. J. Smereka, "De Senecae Tragoediis Dinosis Colore Fucatis," *Eos* 32 (1929) 615-650.

[26] She may also hurl the corpse of her son down to Iason, but cf. below, p. 50.

Both the *Phaedra* and the *Oedipus* feature onstage suicides, of Phaedra and Iocasta respectively. Like the suicide in Sophocles' *Ajax*, both of these involve falling on a sword. The *Phaedra* has a scene in which Theseus tries to fit together the dismembered chunks of his son's corpse, with only limited success (1256ff.), that recalls a similar event at the end of Euripides' *Bacchae*.

The *Oedipus* contains an amazing scene. At 299ff. Tiresia instructs Manto:

> *appellite aris candidum tergo bovem*
> *curvoque numquam colla depressam iugo.*
> *tu lucis inopem, nata, genitorem regens*
> *manifesta sacri signa fatidici refer.*

Then Manto describes to the blind seer what is being transacted onstage.[27] First (306ff.):

> *MANTO*
> *iam tura sacris caelitum ingressi focis.*
> *TIRESIA*
> *quid flamma? largas iamne comprendit dapes.*
> *MANTO*
> *subito refulsit lumine et subito occidit.*

She then describes (321ff.) the baleful and frightening appearance of the fire on the altar. Next (337ff.) the bull and heifer are slaughtered. Their struggles and the effusion of blood are graphically described. Then Manto removes and inspects the entrails, finding all sorts of dire portents. Even so, the slaughtered animals continue to twitch (376ff.):

> *membra cum gemitu movet,*
> *rigore tremulo debiles artus micant,*
> *infecit atras lividus fibras cruor, etc.*

---

[27] At one point (*op. cit.* 56-63) Zwierlein fixes on various passages in which stage business is accompanied by *narratio* describing what the audience should be able to see for itself. He mentions such passages as *Tr.* 945ff. and 999ff., *Ag.* 775ff., *H.F.* 104ff., *Ph.* 583ff. and 704ff. but, remarkably, not this passage, the most conspicuous of them all. But although such passages cannot be matched with passages from Greek tragedy, they are not necessarily disturbing in stage plays. Something very similar can occasionally be seen in Roman comedy (for instance at Plautus, *MG* 200ff.). Also, such passages contain implicit stage directions. Some, at least, are expressions of the profoundly rhetorical nature of Senecan tragedy and as such are opportunities for colorful description too good to miss. Protracted dumb-show such as would otherwise occur would be alien to the spirit of ancient tragedy, and at least one reason that these passages cannot be matched by Greek examples is that a number of them describe categories of action that do not occur on the Greek stage. Then too, the possibility that Seneca included in his plays passages such as these that are eminently suitable for recitation is by no means inimicable to the theory that the plays in which they occur were written for stage production.

From the surrounding context there can be no doubt that Manto is describing an onstage sacrifice. How could such a scene be staged?

In the first place, it would be easy for the actor playing Manto to toss in the flames some substance—possibly sulphur (cf. *Me.* 824ff.)—at the moment he announces he is placing incense on the altar. This would produce an impressive gout of flame and smoke. The sacrifice of the animals cannot of course have been real. To be sure, in an age of the world in which a popular mime featured an onstage crucifixion,[28] the onstage killing of animals might not have offended the tastes of some theatergoers, shaped by the spectacles. But such an onstage slaughter would have been too unpredictable and the chances of disrupting a dramatic performance too great.[29] Probably the safest way of staging this scene would have been to bring onstage a couple of calves suitably drugged, and to kick their legs out from under them at the moment of sacrifice. Then artificial blood could be squirted about as desired and some offal could be used to represent the innards inspected by Manto.

At first this suggestion may seem far-fetched. Three points may be mentioned in its defense. First, the staging of this scene could easily be facilitated by having a bevy of extras cluster about the altar, concealing from the audience whatever manipulations and equipment would be needed. Second, it has been pointed out that the use of performing animals in the spectacles implies that the art of animal training must have been cultivated to a high degree. And indeed, the use of the cattle here and the dog Cerberus in the *Hercules Furens* may be said to cater to a taste for the spectacular use of animals characteristic of the times.[30] Hence the production of an onstage animal sacrifice would not be beyond the means of the theater of Seneca's age.

In the third place, the text of the play may provide confirmation that the scene was staged in some way such as suggested here. For the description of the struggles of the slaughtered and disembowelled animals may have been inserted since the author assumed the (actually alive) calves might be seen by the audience to be still moving on the ground, and wished to provide a textual justification for any such possible movement.

We have seen that both the *Agamenmo* and the *Thyestes* have ghost-apparitions. The prologue of the *Thyestes* involves a dialogue between the Tantali Umbra and the Furia. Then, evidently, both of these infernal

---

[28] Cf. Appendix I.

[29] For the problems (material but not as insuperable as the author thinks) inherent in bringing animals onstage, cf. Peter D. Arnott, "Animals in the Greek Theater," *G&R* n.s. 6 (1959) 177-179.

[30] Cf. George Jennison, *Animals for Show and Pleasure in Ancient Rome* (Manchester, 1937).

beings pass into the palace, a fine visual metaphor for their infestation of
the House of Pelops. The *Agamemno* also features a moment of visual
spectacle when Strophius enters on his chariot (913ff.).

Another stage-effect probably occurs when Atreus witnesses the
upheaval of the palace in the *Thyestes* (262ff.):

> imo mugit e fundo solum,
> tonat dies serenus ac totis domus
> ut fracta tectis crepuit et moti lares
> vertere vultum.

Unless this is merely Atreus' hallucination, the description would be accompanied at least by suitable sound effects. Also, this detail imitates a
similar phenomenon in Euripides' *Bacchae* and since the suggestion has
been made that that latter event was accompanied by some sort of scenic
effect to represent an earthquake,[31] there is no reason for denying the
possibility that some visual effect was intended to accompany the lines
quoted here. The same effect, or at least a similar one, might have accompanied the description of the burning buildings in the *Medea*, discussed above.[32]

A novel dramatic technique is employed at the beginning of the second
scene of Act IV of the *Agamemno* in which Agamemno and Clytemnestra
enter in a kind of dumb-show. Clytemnestra has no lines to say and
evidently exits right after escorting her husband onstage. This scene,
which looks unprecedented in ancient tragedy, has caused commentators
difficulty and is usually regarded as inept.[33] Another problem at this
point in the play is the awkward series of events regarding Cassandra.
First she falls in a swoon and the chorus rushes to her aid. But they are so
distracted by the entry of the royal couple that they appear to forget her
altogether. After the dumb-show entrance, Agamemno launches into a
speech, and only then spots the prostrate girl and orders his retainers to
pick her up.

In these and other ways the *Agamemno* is without doubt Seneca's least
satisfactory play. R.J. Tarrant has sought to explain the deficiencies of

---

[31] Cf. E.R. Dodds' commentary on the *Bacchae* (2nd ed., Oxford, 1960) 147-149.

[32] For the purposes of this argument it does not matter whether such onstage events as
earthquakes (Aesch., *Prom.*, Eur., *Herac.*, *Ba.*, Naevius, *Lycurgus*, etc.) or fires were
realistically represented or merely conveyed by verbal suggestion, insofar as the problem
is no more urgent regarding Seneca's plays than plays unambiguously written for the
theater. For representative discussions of the problem cf. Peter D. Arnott, *Greek Scenic Conventions in the Fifth Century B.C.* (Oxford, 1962) 123ff. and Oliver Taplin, *The Stagecraft of
Aeschylus* (Oxford, 1977) 34 and 273-275.

[33] So R.J. Tarrant in his 1975 commentary on the play.

this play by the suggestion that it is an imperfect conflation of Greek models:[34]

> The awkward "joins" at 909f., 950, and 1001 suggest that Seneca has grafted scenes involving Cassandra on to a structure originally dominated by Electra.

Perhaps the problems associated with the transition between the two scenes of Act IV are attributable to the same cause.

Other visual effects involving stage business and the use of extras will be discussed in later contexts.

From Vitruvius 5.6.2 and 5.7.2 we know that in the Roman theater the chorus shared the *pulpitum* with the actors rather than occupying the *orchestra*, as in the Greek theater. Doubtless, therefore, dance played little or no role in Senecan drama and the limited number of choral meters used by the poet, as well as the absence of strophic responsion, are to be explained by reference to this fact. However there are some passages which afford scope for physical activity on the part of the chorus. One thinks, for instance, of the entrance of a chorus of roistering merrymakers in the *Hercules Furens* (830ff.), an amoebic lamentative *kommos* by Hecuba and the chorus in the *Troades* (99ff.—the unusually detailed physical description of the chorus is noteworthy), and the epithalamium in the *Medea* (56ff.) as choral passages that may have been accompanied, if not by dance, at least by visually interesting effects.

IV. DRAMATIC TIME

If dramatic performances employ fictitious space, they also use fictitious time. In classical tragedy, however, for the orientation of the audience the playwright is obliged to supply information about dramatic space, but not about time. Many classical plays make no mention of time, probably because in the absence of explicit temporal information the audience is to assume that dramatic time runs parallel to real time during acted episodes, and accepts a convention that at least some choral stasima mark an indeterminate passage of time. But if a playwright wishes, he can provide some information about dramatic time, sometimes partial, sometimes sufficient to establish an elaborate internal time-scheme. Thus, most memorably, the author of the pseudo-Senecan *Octavia* has created an elaborate temporal structure spanning three days, in which events of the first day are paralleled by events on the third. In the absence of the normal structure of a Graeco-Roman tragedy (the

---

[34] Tarrant, *ib.* 16-18 (the quote is from p. 18).

rhythmic alternation of acted episodes and choral stasima) this temporal scheme in fact supplies the basic structure of the play.[35]

Temporal information is supplied in three Senecan plays. In two, a familiar device of Greek tragedy is imitated. Some Greek tragedies, such as Aeschylus' *Agamemnon*, commence at or somewhat before dawn, and daybreak occurs in the course of the play. The reason for this device may be that the plays in question were the first plays in their tetralogies and there is a deliberate confusion of fictitious time and the real time of the performance, since tragic performances would have begun early in the day.[36] Hence, if this surmise is true, the playwrights were taking advantage of the fact that these plays actually did begin before sunrise. Two of Seneca's tragedies, the *Hercules Furens* and the *Oedipus*, imitate this Greek device. We may of course doubt that Seneca employs this device for the same reason. More likely it merely persisted as a special convention.

In the *Hercules Furens* Iuno remarks on the constellations of the winter sky that are visible as she speaks (6ff.). Then at the end of her monologue she says (123f.):

> *clarescit dies*
> *ortuque Titan lucides croceo subit.*

Thus the choral entry that immediately follows assumes the character of an aubade (125ff.):

> *iam rara micant sidera prono*
> *languida mundo; nox victa vagos*
> *contrahit ignes luce renata,*
> *cogit nitidum Phosphoros agmen, etc.*

A similar understanding of fictitious time stands behind the first lines of the *Oedipus*:

> *iam nocte Titan dubius expulsa redit*
> *et nube maestus squalida exoritur iubar, etc.*

The *Agamemno* confronts us with a more developed internal time-scheme. This play also begins in darkness, not the genuine darkness of night but that created by the Umbra Thyestis (34ff.):

> *versa natura est retro;*
> *avo parentem, pro nefas! patri virum,*
> *natis nepotes miscui -- nocti diem.*

---

[35] Cf. Sutton, *op. cit.* 9-20 (after C.J. Herington, "*Octavia Praetexta*: A Survey," *CQ* 11, 1961, 18-20).

[36] This notion, of course suggested by Aeschylus' *Agamemnon*, cannot be extended to dramatic forms other than tragedy in which there is a movement from night to day in the course of the play, such as Aristophanes' *Wasps*.

Only as he disappears from the stage does the Umbra Thyestis command *redde iam mundo diem* (54). So again, for a different dramatic reason, dawn is understood to break at the end of the prologue. A later passage also supplies temporal information (908f.):

> *stat ecce Titan dubius emerito die,*
> *suane currat an Thyestea via.*

Thus the action of this play seems to correspond to the passage of a day. So the *Agamemno* would appear to be the only ancient tragedy that explicitly conforms to the Aristotelian dictum (*Poetics* 5 1449 b 8) that "regarding length, tragedy at most tends to fall within a single revolution of the sun or slightly more." By Seneca's time had his critical dictum become a principle accepted by playwrights? On the other hand, one should recall Tarrant's attractive proposed emendation *e medio die* for *emerito die*.[37] If this is accepted, then the handling of dramatic time in the *Agamemno* would be just as in the *Hercules Furens* and the *Oedipus*.

A kind of temporal framework also exists in the *Hercules Oetaeus*. When he is at Euboea in Act I Hercules orders a sacrifice to be performed to Iupiter (101ff.). Then, after the scene has shifted to Trachin, Hyllus describes the particulars of this sacrifice. So some indeterminate amount of time must be understood to have elapsed between Act I and the rest of the play (also necessary to allow Hercules time for his homeward voyage), coordinated with the shift of settings.

The only other temporal information supplied in Senecan tragedy is at *Oedipus* 37ff. where we are told that the action of the play occurs at the height of summer, in connection with a description of the failing crops of the land of Thebes. By contract, in the prologue of the *Hercules Furens* Iuno stands beneath winter constellations.

According to Zwierlein,[38] attention should be paid to temporal irregularities within acts: the irrational way time is jumped forward. For instance, in the *Troades* Agamemno orders at lines 351f. that Calchas be summoned, and the seer appears immediately. Likewise, at *Oedipus* 299ff. Tiresia orders that victims be brought to the altar, and this command is accomplished as early as line 302.

---

[42] *Op. cit.* (*1975*) 345.

[38] *Op. cit.* 29-38. It will be understood that the major purpose of this section is investigation of Seneca's handling of dramatic time insofar as it has a bearing on the question of whether or not (as has been alleged) Senecan tragedy exhibits temporal anomalies that would tend to establish that these plays were not written for the stage. Critical claims (such as those of Shelton, *op. cit.* 17-25) that in Senecan tragedy the flow of time can be distorted or even iterated are not taken into account according to the assumption that, if these claims have validity, such chronological distortions constitute an acceptable form of artificial dramatic convention and as such have no bearing on the problem at hand.

It is hard to imagine that any significance should be placed on such examples. In the first place, it is in the nature of artificial dramatic time to be more elastic and pliable than real time, and one imagines an audience would accept such pliability as well as any other theatrical convention. In the second, we must take into account the possibility that two lines immediately juxtaposed in a dramatic text may in fact be separated by significant bits of dumb-show. As will be shown below,[39] in the *Oedipus* dumb-show was probably important during the preparations for the sacrifice: the victims and their sacrificers enter at this point and it is easy to imagine this entry staged as an impressive processional.

V. The Actors

A. *Disposition of Roles*

In ancient tragedy no more than three actors were supposed to be employed.[40] According to previous students,[41] Seneca often violated this rule. However we shall see that such violations are considerably fewer than have been claimed.

The easiest way to represent the disposition of roles in an ancient play is by use of diagrams. Those presented here are prepared according to two assumptions. The first is that in addition to speaking actors, the poet had at his disposal non-speaking supernumeraries to represent *personae mutae*.[42] The other is that his actors wore masks, which would facilitate the use of an actor for more than one role during the course of a play and would also allow a character to be played sometimes by a speaking actor, sometimes by a mute supernumerary. Since both mutes and masks were part of the normal appurtenances of the ancient tragic theater, there is no visible reason for denying their availability to Seneca.

The first diagram in this series, included for the reader's convenience, represents the understanding of act-divisions of the various plays adopted for the purpose of the present study.[43] To be sure, not all authorities

---

[39] Cf. below, p. 34.

[40] Horace, *Ars Poetica* 192.

[41] Notably G. Richter in his 1902 Teubner edition and J. Viansino in his edition (Paravia-Turin, 1965); cf. also Zwierlein, *op. cit.* 45-51.

[42] Fantham, *op. cit.* 40, seems not to take this possibility into account. One can criticise (as does Zwierlein, *ib.* 45-47) the decision to make the important part of Polyxena a mute role in the fourth act of the *Troades*, but this is at most an artistic miscalculation. Given two mutes, Act IV of that play is perfectly stageable.

[43] A couple of peculiarities of the following chart ought to be explained. Intervening choral odes are not taken into account (so that the reader can appreciate at a glance the relative lengths of the various acts). And if a choral ode is immediately followed by an entrance cue spoken or sung by the chorus, for a reason explained in a later context the act is reckoned to begin at the point the chorus gives the entrance cue rather than afterwards.

would accept this traditional division of all plays in the Senecan corpus into five acts.[44] But since this question appears to have no bearing on the problems addressed in the present study, the traditional scheme will be followed.

Some of the analysis given here presupposes understandings about entrances and exits that will be discussed in Part II.

The Acts of Seneca's Tragedies

	I	II	III	IV	V
Hercules Furens	1-124	202-523	592-827	893-1052	1138-1344
Troades	1-164	165-370	409-813	861-1008	1056-1178
Medea	1-55	116-300	380-578	670-848	879-1027
Phaedra	1-273	358-735	829-958	989-1122	1154-1280
Oedipus	1-109	202-402	509-708	764-881	911-1061
Agamemno	1-56	108-309	408-585	586-807	867-1012
Thyestes	1-121	176-335	404-545	622-788	885-1112
Hercules Oetaeus	1-232	233-582	700-1030	1128-1517	1603-1006

Hercules Furens

	ACT I	II	III	IV	V
Protagonist	---	Lycus	Hercules	Hercules	Hercules
Deuteragonist	Iuno	Amphitryo	Amphitryo	Amphitryo	Amphitryo
Tritagonist	---	Megara	Theseus	Theseus	Theseus

Viansino thinks that the tritagonist plays Iuno and Megara and that a fourth actor is needed to play Theseus. Evidently this view presumes that a single actor cannot shift between male and female roles, either because of the supposedly limited ability of the actor or because of the extra difficulty of costume-changes implied. But the experience of the Greek theater scarcely supports this view,[45] and the lengths of the choruses separating Acts II-V surely afford ample time for changes of costume.

In Act IV the tritagonist playing Theseus must exit in time to supply Megara's voice from "within the palace."

Megara is onstage during Act III (cf. 626ff.) but is played by a mute supernumerary.

---

[44] See the discussion by Tarrant, *op. cit.* (*1978*) 218-221.
[45] This is true in a number of cases. For example, in Euripides' *Alcestis* the deuteragonist plays Thanatos, Alcestis, Pheres, and Heracles.

Troades

	I	II	III	IV	V
I	---	Pyrrhus	Andromacha	Andromacha	Andromacha
II	Hecuba	Agamemno	Ulixes	Hecuba	Hecuba
III	---	Talthybius *and* Calchas	Senex	Helena	Nuntius

Alternatively the protagonist could play Pyrrhus, Ulixes, and Hecuba, and the deuteragonist could play Agamemno and Andromacha.

The single utterance of Astyanax in Act III (792) is no more problematic than similar child-utterances in Greek tragedies such as Euripides' *Medea*. The Senex is not onstage during the long interview between Andromacha and Ulixes so the tritagonist can speak the boy's line from offstage.

Medea

	I	II	III	IV	V
I	Medea	Medea	Medea	Medea	Medea
II	---	Creo	Iason	---	Nuntius *and* Iason
III	---	Nutrix	Nutrix	Nutrix	Nutrix

Richter and Viansino both have the Nuntius played by the tritagonist in Act V. As the Nuntius exits when the Nutrix enters at line 890, this assignment of roles is impossible.

Phaedra

	I	II	III	IV	V
I	Phaedra	Phaedra	Phaedra	Phaedra	Phaedra
II	Hippolytus	Hippolytus	Theseus	Theseus	Theseus
III	Nutrix	Nutrix	Nutrix	Nuntius	Nuntius

Richter would have Phaedra and Theseus played by the protagonist and only Hippolytus by the deuteragonist. But it would appear sounder practice to protect, when possible, the protagonist from the necessity of playing multiple roles.

Oedipus

	I	II	III	IV	V
I	Oedipus	Oedipus	Oedipus	Oedipus	Oedipus
II	Iocasta	Creo	Creo	Iocasta and Phorbas	Iocasta
III	---	Manto	---	Senex	Nuntius
IV	---	Tiresia	---	---	---

In Act IV the fourth actor could of course play Phorbas. But in that act Iocasta must make an unmarked exit[46] soon after her last line (at 880f. we learn she is in the palace) and it looks as if this exit may be made in order to free the deuteragonist for the role of Phorbas.

Agamemno

	I	II	III	IV	V
I	---	Clytemnestra	Clytemnestra	Clytemnestra	Clytemnestra
II	Thyestis Umbra	Aegisthus	---	Agamemno	Stropheus and Aegisthus
III	---	Nutrix	Eurybates	Cassandra	Cassandra
IV	---	---	---	---	Electra

Thyestes

	I	II	III	IV	V
I	---	---	Thyestes	---	Thyestes
II	Tantali Umbra	Atreus	Atreus	---	Atreus
III	Furia	Satelles	Tantalus	Nuntius	---

Hercules Oetaeus

	I	II	III	IV	V
I	Hercules	Deianira	Deianira	Hercules	Philoctetes and Hercules
II	Iole	Nutrix	Nutrix	Alcmena	Alcmena
III	---	---	Hyllus	Hyllus	Hyllus

[46] Zwierlein, *op. cit.* 52-56, dwells on what we shall call uncued entrances and exits, as if the presence of such uncued movements tells against the idea that Seneca was writing for the stage. But in Part II we shall see that such uncued movements are rarely if ever baffling to the careful reader.

It is possible to distribute the parts of the *Hercules Oetaeus* among three actors and the idea of previous editors that a fourth actor is required for the part of Hyllus may be set aside. But the protagonist is required to play several roles—two in one act—and the tritagonist is given remarkably little to do (although the same might be said of the protagonist in the *Thyestes*). This would appear to represent a different and less able dramatic technique than that found in Seneca's genuine plays.

In the *Phoenissae* sketches it is possible to distribute the parts so that the protagonist plays Iocasta and perhaps Oedipus, the deuteragonist plays Antigone and Polynices, and the tritagonist plays Oedipus (if the protagonist does not), the Satelles, and Eteocles.

So five of the genuine plays in the Senecan corpus (as well as both the *Hercules Oetaeus* and the *Octavia*) adhere to the three-actor rule and two do not. This fact scarcely constitutes evidence that Seneca was not writing for the stage, for several reasons. First and foremost, an examination of Seneca's part-distributions and handling of actors shows that he invariably follows sound dramaturgic principles: have the same character played by the same actor, engineer your entrances and exits so as to leave ample time for costume changes, try to protect your protagonist from the distracting duty of playing multiple rules, etc. Indeed, a writer who followed the letter of the three-actor law but violated such principles as these would create much greater suspicion that he was not writing for production. In the second place, despite Horace's injunction, the three-actor rule was not followed in Roman comedy and we really have no idea how uniformly it was obeyed in prior Roman tragedy: after all, a rule that had originated in classical Athens for a practical purpose—the limited number of competent actors available—was now no more than a literary convention. Finally, it may in fact be the case that the classical Greek tragedians themselves occasionally violated this rule, or at least that an attentive Roman student of their plays would think they did. For there are some Greek tragedies, such as Sophocles' *Oedipus Coloneus*, where we are faced with a choice: either concede the use of a fourth actor or think that one character is played by more than one actor during the course of the play (in the same way, some of the earlier Greek tragedies employing the tritagonist, such as Sophocles' *Ajax*, provide precedent for the under-utilization of the three actors in the *Thyestes*).[47]

---

[47] Cf. the analysis of part-divisions in Sophocles' *Oedipus Coloneus* given by Flickinger, *op. cit.* 180.

B. *Mutes, Extras, and Children*

Besides actors, and of course the chorus, ancient drama had at its disposal other human resources: mute supernumeraries, various sorts of extra, and children. All of these categories are represented in Senecan drama.

We have just seen that the parts in Seneca's plays can only be distributed among three or at most four actors according to the assumption that mute supernumeraries were also available: Megara in Act III of the *Hercules Furens*, Polyxena and Pyrrhus in Act IV of the *Troades*, Orestes and Pylades in Act V of the *Agamemno* and also, for that matter, Lichas in Acts I and II of the *Hercules Oetaeus* (cf. lines 99 and 567f.).

In his tragedies Seneca regularly employs extras. Sometimes their presence and identity are explicitly attested when they are identified as *famuli, famulae,* or *milites.* In other passages their presence can be deduced from the fact that a character issues a command with an otherwise inexplicable imperative. The commonest use of extras is as house slaves or as the retinue of kings and similar exalted persons. Often they are commanded to bring something, or even a person, on or off the stage, or to open a door, so that they seem to function almost as visible stagehands.

In the *Hercules Furens* Lycus calls upon his followers to burn down the temple in which Amphitryo and Megara have taken refuge (506ff.). For some reason not explained in the text this order is not carried out. However at 616f. Hercules says:

> sed templa quare miles infestus tenet
> limenque sacrum terror armorum obsidet?

Either one soldier has been left behind, or this is poetic singular-for-plural and the soldiers addressed at 506ff. are still onstage.

At lines 893f. of the same play the chorus sings:

> stantes, sacrificus, comas
> dilecta tege populo

So a sacrificial priest must be onstage. Immediately thereafter Hercules enters and gives orders that sacrificial victims be brought onstage (908ff.). Again, this command is evidently not carried out. To whom is this order given? One thinks of assistants to the priest, or perhaps the palace slaves whom Amphitryo orders take away Hercules' weapons at 1053.

The comings and goings of these extras in the *Hercules Furens* will be traced more carefully in connection with the examination of entrances and exits in Part II.

In the *Troades* Ulixes orders his retinue to hunt for Astyanax (617f.) and subsequently he bids them break into the tomb of Hector (679f.). The following lines between Ulixes and Andromacha must be spoken as these extras attack the stage building. The same occurs in the *Medea* when Iason bids his soldiers attack the palace as Medea makes her way to the roof (980f.). Shortly thereafter, he bids them set it afire. Extras are also used in Act II of the *Medea* when Creo bids his *famuli* keep Medea away from him.

At *Me*. 843 Medea, evidently alone onstage, gives the order *huc natos voca*. Whom is she addressing? Perhaps the Nutrix emerges just in time to receive this order, goes in, gets the children, and is represented as escorting them to their new stepmother bearing the fatal gifts. Alternatively, perhaps, some retainer, maybe a paedagogue, is onstage to receive this command.

At the beginning of the *Phaedra* Hippolytus orders his fellow huntsmen to go to various places. This is the only passage in Senecan tragedy which gives us an idea of how many extras might have been available. If one allows an extra for each singular imperative and two for every plural imperative, it would seem that twelve extras are onstage. This mode of reckoning may strike the reader as over-literal. However, the passage would seem silly if only two or three extras were present. Therefore we may assume a significantly larger number.

Several times in the course of the play the palace servants are given instructions. At 387ff. Phaedra bids her *famulae*—the only female extras in Seneca—remove her costly robes. At 725ff. she bids *famuli* come protect her from Hippolytus' rape. At 863 Theseus commands them—or perhaps his own retinue—to open the door of the palace, and at 884 he bids these same extras bind Phaedra. At 1247 extras are commanded to bring the bloody chunks of Hippolytus' corpse, and at 1275 they are told to open the palace door.

Extras must be used in the sacrifice scene of the *Oedipus*. The order to produce the victims given at 299f. must be carried out. A sacrificial priest must be present and, as suggested above, a number of extras grouped about the altar might facilitate the staging of the scene, and also help make it visually impressive. Later in the play (707f.) Oedipus gives orders that Creo be locked in a rocky dungeon. Possibly he has a retinue of soldiers, or else this order is given to the slaves who are commanded to go fetch Phorbas at lines 823f.

Extras are twice mentioned in Act IV of the *Agamemno*. *Famuli* are told to lift up the swooning Cassandra at 787 and the *fida famuli turba* is commanded at line 800 to restrain Cassandra until her frenzy passes. In the next act the slaves are told to take Electra away (997). And in the *Thyestes* the *turba famularis* is ordered to open the doors of the palace to reveal the banqueting Thyestes within.[48]

Extras are used in two acts of the *Hercules Oetaeus*. At 101ff. Hercules orders some people—he uses a plural imperative—to drive sacrificial animals to the temple. Presumably he is accompanied by retainers. Later in the play, when Hercules has collapsed, Alcmena bids some extras, presumably palace slaves, remove the hero's weapons. This looks like an imitation of a similar transaction in the *Hercules Furens*.[49]

Extras serve to make the scenes in which they appear more visually impressive, by augmenting the number of individuals on the stage. They are also available for various kinds of interesting stage business.

The use both of mutes and extras is redolent of the stage. This is especially so of the use of extras who are not identified in the text. As with characters who are not verbally identified, it would seem as if the author were relying on visual cues to identify them to the audience.

A third category of supernumerary consists of children: Astyanax in the *Troades*, and the children killed in the *Hercules Furens, Medea*,[50] and *Thyestes* (that the children are brought onstage is shown by *Th.* 492f.). As noted earlier, the only line spoken by a child, *Tr.* 792, is in all probability spoken by an offstage actor.

The number of child parts in Senecan tragedy leads to the incidental observation that the killing of children is remarkably common in Seneca: one or more children are killed in four out of the seven authentic plays.

VI. THE CHORUS

A. *Identity*

In some of the tragedies of the Senecan corpus the identity, age, or even sex of the chorus is not stated. This has led one recent commentator to state that *Il Coro delle tragedie senecane non é un personaggio e no puo essere giudicato come tale.*[51] For the same reason, another modern scholar has asserted with specific reference to the *Hercules Furens* that ''...the identity of this chorus is not defined in terms of age or nationality, but in terms of its approach to life.''[52] Properly speaking, such critical pronouncements

---

[48] For the way the extras would be used in stage business here cf. William M. Calder III, ''*Secreti Loquimur*: An Interpretation of Seneca's *Thyestes*,'' *Ramus* 12 (1983) 187.

[49] *H.F.* 1053. For a similar imitation regarding Hercules' entrance cue, cf. below, p. 45. n. 7.

[50] Unless one child is replaced by a dummy. Cf. below, p. 50.

[51] F. Caviglia in his commentary on the *Hercules Furens* (Rome, 1979) 75f.

[52] Jo-Ann Shelton in her commentary on the *Hercules Furens* (Göttingen, 1978) 40f.

should only be possible for those who regard Seneca's plays as written for reading or recitation. For if a tragic chorus is to appear in a stage play, it must appear under some definite persona, and if such a persona is not established verbally we must rest content with the assumption that it is intended to be established by visual means. Possibly we should assume that Seneca adopted a convention whereby, unless stated otherwise, the chorus is understood to consist of citizens of the city where the play is sited.[53] Then too, we had better keep in mind a tendency that has been observed in Greek tragedy to employ female choruses in plays with dominant female characters.[54]

In any event, pronouncements such as the first of those quoted here manage to ignore the fact that in the texts of some Senecan tragedies the identity of the chorus is explicitly stated. The chorus of the *Troades* is composed of captive Trojan women. This is shown by two statements addressed to the chorus by Hecuba, 65 *turba captivae mea* and 83 *fidae casus nostri comites*. In the *Oedipus* lines 124f. show that the chorus consists of Theban citizenry:

> *stirpis invictae genus interimus,*
> *labimur saevo rapiente fato;*

The chorus of the *Agamemno* is shown to be made up of Mycenaeans by 350f.:

> *tua te colimus*
> *turba Mycenae.*

On the basis of the second stasimon (310ff.) it is generally thought that the chorus is composed of women.[55]

Then too, several plays contain physical descriptions of the chorus: the primary chorus of the *Troades* (63ff.), and the secondary choruses of the *Hercules Furens* (827ff.),[56] *Agamemno* (568ff.) and *Hercules Oetaeus* (119ff.).

In other plays the identity of the chorus is not made explicit (the *iuvenes* of *Me.* 107f. are not the play's chorus but the youth of Corinth, whom the chorus bids indulge in genial hymeneal insults). In such cases, as suggested, the proper conclusion is probably that the chorus is composed of local citizenry, save that because of the strong female interest in the *Medea* and the *Phaedra* local women are likelier.

A question not entirely separate from the establishment of the choral persona is the rationalization of its presence in the play or, more

---

[53] This is true, for example, of the chorus of Euripides' *Alcestis*.

[54] Flickinger, *op. cit.* 138. Cf. also (e.g.) Jebb's introduction to his commentary on Sophocles' *Antigone*, xxvii.

[55] So, e.g., Tarrant, *op. cit.* (*1975*) 231.

[56] For this secondary chorus, cf. below p. 41.

specifically, of its initial entrance in the parodos. This is done in the *Troades*, in which the chorus consists of Hecuba's fellow captives, and in the *Medea*, where it enters celebrating Iason's new marriage. But it is more typical of Seneca not to supply any distinct motive for the chorus' entry. However one should remember that Greek tragedies exist in which no real motive for the choral entry is provided.[57]

In the *Hercules Oetaeus* a secondary chorus of captive maidens appears first. The primary chorus of Aetolian women does not enter until line 583. Its entrance is heralded by Deianira in lines that establish its identity and give a reason for its presence (581f.):

> vos, quas paternis extuli comites focis,
> Calydoniae, lugete deflendam vicem.

The manner in which the chorus is introduced therefore seems to represent a technique that differs from Seneca's.

B. *Onstage Presence*

In some plays the chorus does not converse in dialogue with the actors through the medium of the coryphaeus (first chorister and choral spokesman), and the fact that some choral odes have little to do with the surrounding dramatic context is notorious in Senecan criticism.[58] Then too, there are passages in which characters plot foul deeds in the presence of the chorus without extracting an oath of secrecy or at least enjoining silence on it. These facts, taken in combination with the absence of the normal concluding choral *Schlusswort* of Greek tragedy, have prompted suggestions that in at least some Senecan plays the chorus exits during the acted episodes or at least retires "to the back of the stage"[59] and is not to be thought of as present for the episodes.

The allegation that some Senecan choral odes are of dubious relevance is a problem of literary criticism outside the scope of the present study. But in order to lay to rest the notion that the chorus is withdrawn during the acts it is worth pointing out that on a number of occasions the chorus is demonstrably onstage during episodes. This is obvious in cases where

---

[57] Cf. Flickinger, *op. cit.* 150.

[58] The classic discussion of this problem is W. Mark, *Funktion und Form der Chorlieder in den Seneca-Tragödien* (diss. Hamburg, 1932) 6ff. Cf. also Ulrich von Wilamowitz, *Heracles* I² 12, 13, Calder, *op. cit.* (*1975*) 32-35, Shelton, *op. cit.* 40-44, and Zwierlein, *op. cit.* 76-80.

[59] Shelton, *ib.* 41 n. 4 (in the context of the Roman theater, what precisely does "to the back of the stage" mean?) The allegation that the chorus leaves the stage has been made by William M. Calder III, "Seneca: Tragedian of Imperial Rome," *CJ* 71 (1976) 6 (cf. also his *op. cit.* (*1975*)) and by Tarrant, *op. cit.* (*1978*) 223-228.

the chorus does engage in dialogue with an actor or (a rather frequent scene in Seneca) in which a Nuntius or similar eyewitness describes an offstage event to the chorus. It is less obvious but nonetheless true in another type of situation. One assumes that if the chorus were to leave the stage or at least retire to the back and become disconnected from the dramatic action, this would occur at the end of a choral passage before the commencement of the next act. Indeed, in such a case the departure of the chorus would technically constitute the beginning of the following act. But consider a passage such as *H.F.* 198ff.:

> venit ad pigros cana senectus,
> humilique loco sed certa sedet
> sordida parvae fortuna domus;
> alte virtus animosa cadit.
> sed maesta venit crine soluto
> Megara parvum comitata gregem,
> tardusque senio graditur Alcidae parens.

In this passage the actual choral ode ends at 201. Lines 202ff. are an entrance cue that signals the beginning of the following act. Thus, since the act really begins at 202, the chorus has lost the opportunity of leaving before its commencement. Hence we may take it as axiomatic that if any choral stasimon concludes with an entrance cue given by the chorus, the chorus must be onstage for the ensuing act.

The correctness of this axiom receives partial verification in the case of the *Agamemno*. If both the primary chorus of the play and the secondary chorus of Trojan captives were portrayed by the same chorus—that is to say, by the same choristers appearing under different personae—it would be necessary, first, to withdraw the primary chorus allowing sufficient time for a change of costume and, second, to repeat the process in order to let the primary chorus reappear. In this case, if ever, Seneca would have had a powerful motive for withdrawing a chorus during an act. But this does not occur. In the first place, the chorus speaks an entrance cue for Eurybates at 408ff. and Eurybates addresses the chorus at line 392c. Then too, the coryphaeus of the secondary chorus speaks his last lines at 775ff. and even if we were to assume that the chorus makes an immediate exit (although this is very improbable, as the chorus more likely leaves with Cassandra at the end of Act IV), there is scarcely time for changing costumes before the entry of the primary chorus at 808. So at the point where Seneca has the best of reasons for withdrawing a chorus, he demonstrably does not. As will be shown below, this observation also holds good for the *Hercules Furens*.

The chorus is attested to be onstage in the following acts: *Hercules*

Furens, Act II (entrance cue at 202ff.) and Act III (dialogue[60] with Amphitryo at 1032ff.); *Troades*, Act II (dialogue with Talthybius at 166f.); *Medea*, Act V (dialogue with the Nuntius at 881, etc.); *Phaedra*, Act II (dialogue with the Nutrix at 358f. and 404f.), Act III (entrance cue at 829ff.), Act IV (entrance cue at 909ff.), and Act V (dialogue with Theseus at 1244ff. and 1256ff.); *Oedipus*, Act II (dialogue with Oedipus at 205) and Act V (dialogue with the Nuntius and with Oedipus at 1004ff. and 1040ff. respectively); *Agamemno*, Act III (entrance cue at 408ff.) and Act IV (secondary chorus with Cassandra); *Thyestes*, Act IV (dialogue with the Nuntius at 626, etc.). Only in the *Hercules Oetaeus* is the chorus withdrawn, for a special reason: it is withdrawn after the parodos to mark a change of scene and only enters under a different persona for the second stasimon, which consequently becomes a sort of second parodos. The chorus is demonstrably onstage for Act III (entry cue at 700ff., and Deianira's speech at 706ff. answers the chorus' question at 703). Short choral passages are interspersed in Act IV (1151, etc.) and the chorus engages in dialogue with Philoctetes in Act V. This play ends with a choral passage (1983ff.).

Thus the chorus can be shown to be onstage for at least one act of each play. It will be appreciated that a dialogue with a Nuntius or herald, named or unnamed, is the commonest situation in which the chorus becomes actively involved during an acted episode. Most choral dialogues are with Nuntii and Nutrices, perhaps because of a feeling that *humiles* should converse with their peers more often than with their betters.

This leaves the question of characters plotting in the presence of the chorus without extracting promises or oaths of silence, as conspirators do in Greek tragedy:[61] in these cases why should the chorus not divulge the secrets they overhear (and hence foil the plots in question) unless the chorus is withdrawn from the stage at such points?

The passages in question are *Ag.* 108ff. where Clytemnestra enters and in a monologue ponders whether Agamemnon ought to be killed by sword or poison, and *Thyestes*, Act II, in which Atreus reveals to the Satelles his plan to kill Thyestes.

Ag. 108ff. is really like a series of passages discussed by Zwierlein[62] in which a character enters and delivers a monologue not heard by other characters on the *pulpitum*: examples are Lycus' monologue at *H.F.*

---

[60] For the purpose of this analysis "dialogue" is defined as any situation in which one character addresses, or clearly speaks within earshot of, another character or the chorus, no matter whether the second character (or the chorus) does or does not respond.

[61] For this practice, cf. also Flickinger, *op. cit.* 155f.

[62] *Op. cit.*, 67-72.

332ff. and Hercules' monologue, *ib*. 592ff. In reality such non-overheard monologues are merely an extension of the dramatic device of the aside.[63] If they prove anything at all, they go to show that the Senecan *pulpitum* was large enough that such passages would not seem silly. In the same way, as we shall see, the *pulpitum* was large enough that Agamemno and Clytemnestra could enter in the *Agamemno* without immediately seeing Cassandra, and large enough that Theseus is obliged to command that Hippolytus' corpse be brought to his part of the stage in the *Phaedra*.[64] But more likely the non-overheard monologue, like the aside of Roman comedy from which it is derived, is an artificial convention of the Senecan stage.[65]

With regard to the interview between Atreus and the Satelles in the *Thyestes*, the assumption that this conversation is not overheard by the chorus deserves to be questioned. Consider the chorus' utterance at 339ff.:

> *quis vos exagitat furor,*
> *alternis dare sanguinem*
> *et sceptrum scelere aggredi?*
> *nescitis, cupidi arcium,*
> *regnum quo iaceat loco.*

This sentiment seems very appropriate for a chorus that indeed has overheard the foregoing dialogue. The problem lies in the first lines of this choral ode (336ff.):

> *tandem regia nobilis,*
> *antiqui genus Inachi,*
> *fratrum composuit minas.*

But since these lines appear to contradict 339ff. (according to which the fraternal strife seems to be continuing rather than to be resolved, as 336ff. indicate) G. Richter in his Teubner edition may well have been

---

[63] *Ib*. 63-67.

[64] Cf. below, pp. 61f.

[65] The words of Beare, *op. cit.* 178, are well worth quoting:

Roman drama owed what success it achieved not to the craft of the scene-painter but to the art of the dramatist and actor. That art was exercised according to the conventions of the ancient theater, conventions accepted almost unconsciously by the contemporary audience, yet puzzling and surprising to the reader of another age and country.

One such convention enunciated by Beare (p. 182) was that "A grand principle of the stage was that a character saw and heard only what the dramatist meant him to see and hear." It is possible to write a fair amount of nonsense about Senecan tragedy by failing to concede that the poet took advantage of dramatic conventions the same as or at least (as with non-overheard monologues, which we have seen to be an extension of the conventional "aside") developed from those used by other ancient playwrights.

right to delete lines 336-338 from the text. So all in all neither plotting-passage gives strong support to the idea that the chorus was withdrawn during the acts of Senecan drama.

C. Secondary Choruses

We have already seen that the *Agamemno* has a secondary chorus of Trojan captives who accompany Cassandra, and that this is a genuine second chorus rather than the same choristers appearing with a new identity. It remains to show that a secondary chorus is also employed in the *Hercules Furens*.[66]

In arguing against the contention that the chorus was withdrawn from the stage during the course of the acts of Senecan tragedies, we neglected the sole passage that might seem to support this view, *H.F.* 827ff.:

> *densa sed laeto venit*
> *clamore turba frontibus laurum gerens*
> *magnique meritas Herculis laudes canit.*

Obviously this passage is an entrance cue, and so at first sight it looks as if the chorus must have been withdrawn for the act preceding this passage. Technically this view is possible, inasmuch as the chorus cannot be proven to be onstage during the act in question. However there is no visible reason why the chorus should be withdrawn at that point. And it seems intrinsically more probable that *H.F.* 827ff. ought to be compared to *Ag.* 586ff., the entry cue for the secondary chorus of the *Agamemno*:

> *sed ecce, turba tristis incomptae comas*
> *Iliades adsunt, quas super celso gradu*
> *effrena Phoebas entheas laurus quatit.*

So *H.F.* 827ff. seems the entry cue for a secondary chorus. The other choruses of the *Hercules Furens* are thoughtful and interlarded with truisms. But the choral ode at *H.F.* 830ff. is a cheerful hymn of triumph praising Hercules, that marks the high point of his career (ironically, since his tragedy begins in the following act). Since the emotional tone of this passages differs so much from that of the play's other choral odes, it is especially plausible that it might be performed by a chorus having a different identity. One thinks of a laurel-garlanded band of youthful merry-makers (864 *sera nos illo referat senectus* could equally well be said by youths or old men).

We may assume that this secondary chorus leaves with the priest and extras (and probably also with Theseus) as they are frightened off by the onset of Hercules' madness. And if the original chorus were withdrawn

---

[66] Cf. *AJP* 105 (1984) 301-305.

for the act preceding 830ff. in order to appear with a new persona, and again were to exit for the same reason, the point at which it would enter for the final time would be at the beginning of the stasimon at 1054ff. Yet the coryphaeus engages in dialogue with Amphitryo at 1032ff. Hence, like the *Agamemno*, the *Hercules Furens* genuinely requires two choruses.

It will be appreciated that it is a feature of Senecan technique to establish the identity of secondary choruses textually and also to rationalize their presence in the play, albeit this is not always done for the primary choruses.

Seneca's use of these secondary choruses poses an obvious problem:[67] the awkwardness of having the primary chorus onstage and silent during their presence. While this difficulty would be undeniably visible in stage production, there are mitigations. In the first place, there are situations in the Greek theater in which two choruses are simultaneously onstage. One such instance is in the *Supplices* of Aeschylus. Most editors think that the play ends with a kind of lyric dialogue between the chorus of Suppliants and a secondary chorus of Handmaidens: if so, how long has this latter chorus been onstage silent before the exodus of the play?

In the second place, in the celebratory scene of the *Hercules Furens* the simultaneous presence of two choruses, later augmented by extras for the interrupted sacrifice, lends the scene extra visual impressiveness. For that matter, while the primary chorus is undoubtedly "under foot" during the scene between Cassandra and the Trojan captives, the presence of two choruses may have been intended to impart extra visual impact to the subsequent entry of Agamemno and Clytemnestra. A third mitigating consideration is that we may not have to think that a Senecan chorus was necessarily as large as the chorus of a Greek tragedy.[68] Thus the simultaneous presence of two choruses (and, in one case, extras) need not imply an intolerably large number of individuals on the stage.

Two choruses are also found in the *Hercules Oetaeus*. We have already seen that one set of choristers would serve for both the secondary chorus of captive maidens that appears in Act I and for the primary chorus of Aetolian women used for the remainder of the play. It is worth noting that the author of this play has imitated Senecan practice by giving his secondary chorus a definite identity, even describing its appearance at 119ff.

---

[67] Cf. Zwierlein, *op. cit.* 80-87.

[68] A. Körte, *NJB für kl. Alt.* 3 (1900) 86 n. 5, followed by J.B. O'Connor, *Chapters in the History of Actors and Acting in Ancient Greece* (Chicago, 1908) 14f., W. Dörpfeld and E. Reisch, *Das griechische Theater*[2] (Aalen, 1966) 261, and Calder, *op. cit. (1975)*. It is also worth pointing out that if the chorus of at least the first part of Ezechiel's *Exagoge* consisted of the daughters of Raguel, that chorus would have numbered six or seven (cf. H. Jacobson, *The Exagoge of Ezechiel*, Cambridge U.K., 1983, 32 with reference to *Ez.* 59—the evidence given by Körte could have been adduced in support of a chorus of seven).

PART TWO

INTERNAL STAGE DIRECTIONS

Introduction

Production criticism is facilitated by the presence of various kinds of information and instructions incorporated into the texts of ancient plays that reveal the authors' intentions and in effect constitute their directions for the staging of their plays. In previous portions of this study some kinds of implicit stage directions have already been examined. Certain textual elements that arguably, but not definitely, represent implicit stage directions are passed over here,[1] as are passages that describe the physical appearance of characters and the chorus,[2] or that suggest the use of "props," although the interest of such information to the stage director would be obvious. This portion of the present study is devoted to the four most significant kinds of implicit stage direction (other, of course, than information about the stage setting): entrance cues, exit cues, verbal cues that identify new characters for the audience, and implicit directions for stage business.

In this context it is necessary to define entrance and exit cues. Actual such cues are explicit statements to the effect that "here comes Oedipus" or "there goes Agamemnon," possibly coupled with some information about the reason for the indicated arrival or departure, or (in the case of entrances) coupled with a cue that identifies a new character. For some reason, it is a frequent feature of Senecan technique to link an entrance cue with information about the entering character's physical appearance.[3] But it would obviously become stultifying to identify each entrance or exit with a crudely explicit cue. Textually, the arrival or departure of a character can equally well be marked with a strong entry or exit line that serves as a relatively unambiguous indicator of that character's movements. However it is characteristic of Senecan technique that not all entrances and exits are textually marked. To a casual

---

[1] Other kinds of implicit stage direction exist. Consider, for example, pronouns. When, for instance, at *H.F.* 6, 8, 10 and 14 Iuno says *hinc...hinc...illinc...hinc* these words may be supposed to be accompanied by demonstrative gestures. And of course pronouns that might strike a reader as unclear or ambiguous regarding their references would be quite clear if accompanied by gestures.

[2] As at, e.g., *H.F.* 202ff. (Amphitryo and Megara), 329ff. (Lycus), and 827ff. (the secondary chorus).

[3] The instances given in the previous footnote illustrate this.

reader there are occasions when characters seem suddenly and perhaps irrationally to materialize or evanesce.[4] But in such cases a reader can at least usually deduce the likely points when such characters enter or leave.

Especially in the absence of stage directions for the reader or a programme for the theatergoer, it is necessary to identify new characters as they appear. Usually this is done verbally in passages that are here called identification cues. Sometimes this is not done, and in such cases we must assume that identification is supposed to be achieved by visual means. As it happens, this assumption is not difficult to make, since characters not identified verbally in their first appearance are individuals who, we may reasonably suppose, could be recognized on the basis of distinctive masks, costumes, or "props." One must admit that this last statement does not apply to those choruses not given an explicit identity in the text. The suggestion has therefore been made[5] that in such cases the audience was to assume that the chorus represent citizens or citizenesses of the city where the scene is set.

The fact that the characters who are not identified in the text on their first appearance happen to be characters who, one may reasonably suppose, could readily be identified by means of visual information tells strongly in favor of the theory that Seneca was writing for the stage. According to the theory that he was writing for reading or recitation, the absence of universal identification cues would be hard to explain. The same comment applies to the poet's handling of textually unidentified extras who must have been identifiable by visual means alone, as discussed in Part One.[6]

The Plays

Hercules Furens

A. *Entrance cues*. The following entrances of characters are clearly marked in the text; sometimes such entrance cues are coupled with other kinds of information such as an identification cue, a rationalization of the entrance, or a physical description of the entering character: entrances of Megara and Amphitryo (202ff.), Lycus (329ff.), Hercules (523), the secondary chorus (827ff.). Other entrances are textually unmarked: Theseus at 592 and Hercules at 895. And, as noted in discussing exits, in a couple of cases it is unclear whether a character stays onstage during choral odes; if not, that character's reentrance after the ode is unmarked.

---

[4] This feature is dwelt on by Zwierlein, *op. cit.* 52-56.
[5] Above, pp. 36.
[6] Above, pp. 33-35.

Especially interesting is the entrance cue (and identification cue) for Hercules at 523. By a remarkable stroke, he is identified by the sound of his approaching tread and his entrance is heralded. Then a choral ode interposes before his entrance at 592.[7] But Theseus, who enters with him, is not acknowledged to be present by the text until line 639.

B. *Exit cues.* Some exits are textually marked and dramatically justified: that of Lycus at 514f. (to sacrifice)[8] and that of Hercules at 639. Save for Hercules' momentary withdrawal from the stage during the killing scene, all other exits are textually unindicated: Iuno at 124 and Megara at 523. Other exits are more problematic. In the first place, does Amphitryo stay onstage or exit during choral odes at 524ff., 830ff., and 1054ff.? (Obviously the prostrate Hercules remains onstage during this last chorus and we have seen that there is no reason for doubting that the primary chorus stays onstage during the appearance of the secondary chorus).[9] Theseus also presents a difficulty. Although he does not speak during Act IV, he is addressed by Hercules at 913f. Therefore Theseus must exit with Amphitryo at the end of Act III or stay onstage with him during the intervening choral ode. And when does Theseus exit in Act IV? The likeliest answer is that he must make as inconspicuous a withdrawal as possible along with the secondary chorus and the extras at the onset of Hercules' madness. Otherwise the question would arise why Theseus does not intervene to stop the killing of the children and Megara.[10]

Another question concerns Megara and the children in Act III. We have already seen that this act can only be made to conform to the three-actor rule according to the assumption that in it she is played by a mute supernumerary,[11] an assumption that is easy enough to make since she is addressed by Theseus at 640f. but says nothing herself. But when does she exit? She is next heard of in Act IV, when Hercules kills her within

---

[7] Observe the inept imitation of this cue in the *Hercules Oetaeus*, where at lines 1128ff. the chorus exclaims:

> sed quis non modicus fragor
> aures attonitas movet?
> est est Herculeus sonus.

In the *Hercules Furens* it is explicitly stated that the heo is identified by the sound of his tread. Here it is not.

[8] According to Tarrant, *op. cit.* (*1975*) 323 the need to perform sacrifice is a common pretext for Senecan exits; this fits in with the author's unceasing fascination with sacrifices.

[9] Above, pp. 41f.

[10] Zwierlein, *op. cit.* 49 makes the absurd argument that Theseus—not otherwise onstage—is the speaker of *H.F.* 1032ff.: here, if ever, is a mischievous solution to a non-existent problem.

[11] Above, p. 29.

the temple. So she, together with the children, must exit at some intervening point. Since she and the children have been clinging to the altar as a means of avoiding Lycus' wrath, and since at 640f. Theseus announces to her that the danger is now over, in all probability she and the children retire from the stage at this point. There is no reason for them to linger.

If it is relatively easy to trace the comings and goings of the principal characters, those of the extras and the secondary chorus pose more vexatious problems. Lycus' soldiers enter with him and evidently remain onstage at least until 616f., or even until Lycus' defeat (or at least one does).[12] The entrance of the secondary chorus at 830 is accompanied or at least immediately followed by the entrance of a priest mentioned at 893f. and attendants whom Hercules orders to prepare a sacrifice at 909ff. Most likely these extras retire with the secondary chorus, probably frightened off by the onset of Hercules' insanity at 939. But at 1053 Amphitryo orders *famuli* to remove Hercules' weapons. When do these slaves arrive and when do they leave? The same question deserves to be asked about the children onstage for the murder scene (986ff.): at what point do they come onstage? Surely the brief appearance of Cerberus poses no material problem.[13] He is produced onstage in connection with Hercules' first entrance (cf. 603f.). "Cerberus"—maybe a specially gotten-up dog—must be led on a chain by an extra, and after being shown to the audience he is quickly led off.

C. *Identification cues.* Usually the identification of a new character is achieved by combining an identification cue with an entrance cue (as for Megara and Amphitryo at 202ff., Lycus at 329ff., and the secondary chorus at 827ff.). But we have seen that identification cues can come significantly before or after the actual entrance of the character in question, in the instances of Hercules and Theseus described above.[14] Another kind of identification cue is required for the prologue. If a play begins with a monologue of the Euripidean type, the speaker must identify himself. This is done by Iuno in the first line of the play.

In the *Hercules Furens*, as it happens, all entering characters are identified in the text. However this is not true of the primary chorus, as discussed in an earlier context.[15]

D. *Stage business.* Significant stage business postulated by the text of the *Hercules Furens* is as follows:

    1. Megara and Amphitryo take refuge at the altar now if not earlier (355ff.).

---

[12] Above, p. 33.
[13] *Pace* Zwierlein, *op. cit.* 54.
[14] Above, p. 45.
[15] Above, p. 35f.

2. Lycus orders his soldiers burn down the temple with its altar to destroy Megara and Amphitryo—but what actually happens? (503ff.)
3. Cerberus is brought onstage (603).
4. At least one soldier is guarding the temple (616f.).
5. Hercules orders his attendants to prepare a thanksgiving sacrifice—but what actually happens? (908ff.)
6. The killing scene (987ff.); this can be broken down into a series of specific events:
   a. One son is killed onstage (987ff.)
   b. The survivors take refuge in the temple (Megara is already within); Hercules attacks the temple under the delusion that it is Lycus' palace (999ff.).
   c. He goes in; Amphitryo stands by the door and describes the killing (1002ff.).
   d. Hercules reenters (1035ff.).
   e. Amphitryo goes to the altar (1039ff.).
   f. Hercules collapses (1043ff.).
   g. Slaves remove his weapons (1053).
   h. At some point, now or later, the corpses of those slain in the temple must be brought onstage—another task for extras—as Hercules sees them at 1143ff.
7. Hercules' arms are given back to him (1294).
8. Hercules draws his bow and threatens to shoot himself (clearly the Stoic philosopher knew nothing about archery, as this form of suicide must be impractical to the point of absurdity) (1299).
9. He threatens to commit suicide with a sword (1312).
10. Amphitryo and Hercules clasp hands (1319).

Troades

A. *Entrance cues*. Entrance cues are given for the chorus (63ff.), Calchas (351f.), Ulixes (517f.), and Pyrrhus (999). Characters entering on entrance lines are Talthybius (153), Agamemno and Pyrrhus (203), Andromacha (409), Helena (861), and the Nuntius (1055). Other entrances are textually unmarked: the Senex who enters with Andromacha at 409, Astyanax at the same point, Andromacha, Hecuba, and Polyxena, who enter with Helena at 861, and Andromacha and Hecuba at 1056 (if they have left the stage for the preceding choral ode). It should perhaps be added that Hecuba is not onstage between her exit after the *kommos*-like parodos and her entrance at 861. When the chorus addresses her at 858ff., she is present only in their imagination.[16]

B. *Exit cues*. At 812f. Ulixes exits, and he commands his retinue to drag off Andromacha. Simultaneously Astyanax is led to his doom. And at 1008 Pyrrhus leads off Polyxena (it is unclear whether Andromacha and

---

[16] *Pace* Zwierlein, *op. cit.* 52f.

Hecuba temporarily exit for the choral ode at 1009ff., since they reappear in the following act). All other exits are uncued.

Of the uncued exits in the *Troades* only that of the Senex looks problematic. For that matter his entrance is also uncued. But his movements become tolerably clear as soon as it is realized that he is in fact Astyanax' paedagogue. He enters with Andromacha and the boy and exits once his charge is safely ensconced in the tomb so that his duty is discharged (512ff.).

C. *Identification cues*. In the *Troades* some characters are identified in the text as they first appear: Hecuba (36), the chorus (63ff.), Pyrrhus (232), Calchas (351f.), Andromacha (418 and 483f.), Ulixes (517f.), Helena (861ff.), and Polyxena (871). But others are not. When Agamemno enters with Pyrrhus at 203 he is never explicitly identified in the text. Possibly it would be accurate to say that his identity can easily be inferred from the general tenor of his dialogue with Pyrrhus. But it is also likely that he bears a regal sceptre such as Lycus carries in the *Hercules Furens* (*H.F.* 331, 399f.). In just the same way Talthybius is not textually identified in his appearance at 153ff, but we may presume that he carries a herald's wand or some similar badge of office to establish his identity. Other unidentified characters are stock tragic types. We have just seen that the individual called by our manuscripts the Senex is Astyanax' paedagogue and his identity would visually be established both by his age and by the way he hovers protectively about the boy. Tragic Nuntii (such as the one who appears at *Tr.* 1056ff.) are not identified. Possibly Nuntii and Nutrices were identifiable on the basis of special costumes or masks.

D. *Stage business*. Most stage business is concentrated in Act III, the struggle for the possession of Astyanax:

1. Astyanax is placed inside the tomb (503f.).
2. The Senex announces that the tomb door is barred—perhaps this statement is accompanied by the sound effect of a bar dropping in place, since the door would of course be barred from the inside (512).
3. Ulixes dismisses his retinue to search for Astyanax. This is a ruse and probably not very much occurs. It is doubtful that the extras leave the stage, even momentarily (717f.).
4. Ulixes orders his retinue to pull down the tomb. Again, this is a ruse, but evidently they storm the tomb during the ensuing dialogue with Andromacha (678f.).
5. Andromacha rushes towards the tomb but is restrained by extras (681).
6. She throws herself at Ulixes' knees (692).
7. She summons Astyanax from the tomb; perhaps his entrance is preceded by sounds of the door being unbarred (705).
8. Astyanax falls at Ulixes' feet (709).
9. Later he is clinging to Andromacha (793).
10. He is dragged off at the end of the act, as is his mother.

The only other significant stage business is Hecuba's swoon at 949ff. and Polyxena dragged away by Pyrrhus at 1113.

Medea

A. *Entrance cues*. Entrances indicated in the text are those of Creo (178), the Nutrix at 568 (if she has exited for the dialogue between Medea and Iason), Medea (738f.), the children (843), and Medea (891 and 982). Some characters enter on entrance lines: Iason at 431, the Nutrix at 670, the Nuntius at 879, Iason at 978. Textually uncued entrances are those of Medea at 115 (or has she been onstage during the parodos?), and the Nutrix at this same point.

At 843ff. the children are brought onstage, given the fatal gifts, and dismissed. They are next heard of at 945ff. When do they enter? The likeliest answer is immediately at this point in an uncued entrance.[17]

B. *Exit cues*. Cued exits are those of Creo at 298f., when he leaves to attend the wedding, Medea and the Nutrix at 578, to prepare the sacrifice, the children at 848, Medea with the surviving child at 974f., and Medea on the magic chariot at 1022ff. Medea makes an uncued exit at 55, if she leaves the stage during the prologue, although her speech at the beginning of Act II would seem better motivated if she has heard the epithalamium by remaining onstage. She has uncued exits at 298f. (only Creo's departure is noted in the text) and 848. It is not clear from the text whether the Nutrix temporarily withdraws after her speech at 430, to leave Medea and Iason alone for their dialogue.

C. *Identification cues*. The following characters are identified in the text: Medea (8), Creo (178), and Iason (435). The Nutrix is explicitly identified as such in Act III (568), but not in connection with her first appearance in Act II. The Nuntius is unidentified and no identity is stated for the chorus.

D. *Stage business*. In the interview with Creo Medea, crossing the stage, approaches the king and he bids his *famuli* keep her away (186f.). We have seen[18] that her appearance at 380ff. may be on the roof of the stage building, in which case she must exit, descend to the *pulpitum*, and reenter to meet Iason at 445. But significant stage business is chiefly associated with two scenes, the sacrifice to Hecate in Act IV and the killing of the children in Act V.

The events of the sacrifice are:

a. Medea offers various sinister gifts to the goddess (771ff.).

---

[17] *Pace* Zwierlein, *ib.* 54.
[18] Above, p. 17.

    b. She slashes herself and lets her blood drip onto the altar (807ff.).

    c. She poisons the gifts (817ff.).

    d. She summons her children perhaps escorted by the Nutrix or a paedagogue,[19] to take the poisoned gifts to their stepmother (843ff.).

And the sequence of events in Act V is:

    a. Medea kills one child on the *pulpitum* (970ff.).

    b. As she withdraws into her house, Iason enters; quickly taking stock of the situation, he orders his soldiers to attack the house. They obey.

    c. She appears on the roof, holding the second child (981ff.).

    d. Iason sees her leaning over the parapet. He bids his soldiers set fire to the house—but what actually happens? (986)[20]

    e. She kills the other child (1018).

    f. The winged chariot appears and she escapes (1022ff.).

At line 1024, having killed the second child, Medea calls down to Iason *recipe iam natos, parens*. It has been suggested that at this point she throws down the child's body, or even that she has dragged to the roof the body of the child killed at ground level and so hurls down both bodies.[21] But it is by no means certain that line 1024 is meant to be accompanied by any stage business. Medea could simply be taunting Iason: "you may now have back the children whom you tried in vain to save!"

Phaedra

    A. *Entrance cues*. Cued entrances are those of the Nutrix (350), Phaedra (384), Hippolytus (424), Phaedra (583), Theseus (829ff.), Phaedra (864), the Nuntius (989f.), and Phaedra (1156). Other characters enter on entry lines: Phaedra (85), the chorus (358), the Nutrix (829, if she does make an entrance here—see below). There may be an uncued entry of the Nutrix at 719—again, see below.

    The *Phaedra* requires extras in several acts, and it is possible to trace their movements. At the beginning of Act III Phaedra is produced on the *fastigium* and immediately bids her *famulae* take away her robes and finery.[22] Evidently they exit immediately. *Famuli* must enter in response to the Nutrix' cry for help at 725f. and carry off Phaedra shortly thereafter (735). Twice in Act IV Theseus issues commands in the plural im-

---

[19] Above, p. 34.

[20] Above, p. 21.

[21] Cf. Fantham, *op. cit.* 37.

[22] Beare, *op. cit.* 178 points out that toilet-scenes are a frequent variety of interior scene in Roman Comedy. The present scene seems a tragic adaptation of that genre.

perative. Presumably he enters at the beginning of the act accompanied by a retinue. If he exits at the end of the act, they would leave with him. If he does not, then they presumably stay and receive orders (more plural imperatives, noted in the discussion of extras in Part I)[23] given by him in Act V.

B. *Exit cues*. Exit cues are as follows: Hippolytus, as he goes to the woods (81ff.), and as he dashes off in horror (718). Other exits are uncued: Phaedra and the Nutrix at 273, Phaedra at the end of Act III, the Nutrix at 735, and Theseus at 958 if he does not remain onstage during the following choral ode.

A special problem is posed by the Nutrix in Act III. She speaks at 580ff. and again at 719ff. but is silent throughout the interview between Phaedra and Hippolytus. And at 600f. Phaedra orders *si quis est abeat comes* and Hippolytus responds *en locus ab omni liber arbitrio vacat*. This dialogue would appear to imply the dismissal and exit of the Nutrix, but it is obvious from her speech at 719ff. that she knows what has transpired between Hippolytus and her mistress. One imagines the likeliest solution of this seeming problem is that the Nutrix retires somewhat, but the audience is able to see that she conceals herself where she can overhear the conversation. Or else, when Hippolytus tells Phaedra that nobody is present, he is really saying "nobody *who matters* is here—of course this Nutrix of yours does not matter."

C. *Identification cues*. Characters identified in the text are Phaedra (129), Theseus (829ff.), and the Nuntius (989f.). Additionally the Nutrix is textually identified at 178, considerably after her entrance at 85. The persona of the chorus is not stated. Neither is Hippolytus explicitly identified in connection with his appearance in Act I. But his identity would not be unknown to the audience from the tenor of his speech, and one would assume that Hippolytus' identification would be facilitated by the bow or other hunting gear he carries as "props."

D. *Stage business*. Significant stage business in the *Phaedra* is:

1. Phaedra bids her *famulae* remove her robes and other finery. She will dress simply. Presumably there is an onstage change of costume before the extras depart (387ff.).
2. Hippolytus holds Phaedra (588).
3. She throws herself at his knees (666).
4. Hippolytus draws his sword and tries to kill Phaedra at the altar (706ff.).
5. She seizes it (710ff.).
6. As if it is polluted by her touch, he throws the sword away (713).

---

[23] Above, p. 34.

7. Extras, summoned by the Nutrix, bear Phaedra away (725).
8. When the doors of the palace are thrown open, Phaedra is revealed holding a sword. Theseus bids her discard it (866).
9. She turns away from him, hiding her face (886f.).
10. Phaedra enters, again bearing a sword, probably atop the stage building (1154f.).
11. By 1168 the corpse of Hippolytus is brought onstage, presumably by extras mentioned later in this act (1247, 1275). Most likely they enter with Theseus at the beginning of the act in a kind of funeral procession at the same time that Phaedra appears on the roof. This may involve a certain amount of dumb-show during the preceding choral ode.
12. Phaedra falls on the sword and kills herself (1200).
13. Theseus gives an order to the extras (1247): *huc, huc reliquias vehite cari corporis.* Since the corpse is already onstage, *huc* must mean "to this part of the *pulpitum* where I stand."
14. Then he tries to fit together the pieces of the corpse.
15. He gives the corpse certain *suprema dona* (1273).
16. He bids the palace doors be thrown open (1275).

The principal value of this analysis is to reveal the importance of the sword. Surely the sword with which Phaedra appears in Acts IV and V is the same weapon discarded by Hippolytus earlier in the play. On the surface the use of this sword appears silly. In Act V Theseus cannot disarm Phaedra, as she is probably overtly on the roof throughout the act.[24] But why does he fail to wrench it from her at 866? The answer, of course, is that the interest in this sword is predominantly symbolic—and that the symbolism with which it is invested is phallic. Seneca is willing to sacrifice realism in the interest of securing this vivid visual metaphor.

Some think that difficulties surround the production of Hippolytus' corpse in Act V.[25] The corpse is brought on, in the manner suggested, at the beginning of the act. Then, to be sure, after it is apostrophized by Phaedra it is ignored for a while. But this is because everybody's attention is diverted by the suicide. And, as just stated, when Theseus says "bring the corpse here" he only means "to this place on the stage," so this line casts no doubt on the proposition that the corpse has been onstage all along. Also, at 1168f. Phaedra looks at the corpse and asks:

> *Hippolyte, tales intuor vultus tuos*
> *talesque feci?*

But at 1249 Theseus sees it and says *Hippolytus hic est?* Is it not an inconsistency that Phaedra can identify the remains while Theseus cannot? No, it is not. Although the corpse is mangled, Phaedra's lines show that

---

[24] Above, pp. 17f.
[25] Zwierlein, *op. cit.* 15-20.

the face is intact—in point of fact, the mask previously worn by the actor playing Hippolytus may be produced as part of the remains—and Theseus' subsequent question is merely rhetorical, if it is a question at all. Better to repunctuate his words so as to remove the question mark.

Oedipus

A. *Entrance cues*. Cued entrances are those of Creo (202ff.), Tiresia and Manto (288ff.), Phorbas (838ff.), and the Nuntius—actually a *famulus*, as we learn at line 912—at 911f. Other characters enter on entrance lines: Iocasta at 81, the chorus at 110, Oedipus at 201 (if he has left the stage during the preceding choral ode), Creo at 509, Oedipus at 764, Iocasta at 773, and the Senex at 784.

B. *Exit cues*. Textually cued exits are those of Tiresia and Manto, to perform further rites (401f.), Creo to the dungeon and Oedipus to the palace (707f.), and Oedipus to the palace (880). Uncued exits are those of Iocasta at 109, Oedipus at 109 (if he does not stay onstage for the parodos), Oedipus at 401 (if he does not stay onstage for the following choral ode), Iocasta at 783, Phorbas and the Senex at 800, and the Nuntius at 979. Cued exits for the *famuli* who accompany Oedipus are found at 707 and 823.

C. *Identification cues*. With one exception, characters are clearly identified in the text at their first appearance: Oedipus (12), Iocasta (81), the chorus (124), Creo (202ff.), Tiresia and Manto (288ff.), Phorbas (939ff.), and the Nuntius (911ff.). The person identified in our text as the Senex Corinthius is the sole exception. His age is mentioned at 817f. and it is possible, in view of the nature of his message, that he is an elderly herald come from Corinth. If so, then like Talthybius in the *Troades* he may be visually identified by a herald's wand or similar badge of office.

D. *Stage business*. At 71 Oedipus prostrates himself before the altar. If the chorus is describing itself in the third person at 197f. (*turba* is a word occasionally used to designate a Senecan chorus, as at *H.F.* 828), it too falls before the altar.

Most stage business occurs in connection with the onstage sacrifice in Act II, which can be analysed into a series of steps:

1. Tiresia commands the sacrifice (299f.).
2. Extras must guide the victims onstage. A sacrificial priest and a number of helpers enter in formal procession (300).
3. The victims are brought to the altar (303).
4. Manto casts incense on the altar and the fire blazes up (306ff.).
5. The flame grows baleful (321ff.).
6. The victims are sprinkled with meal (336).
7. The bull resists the sacrifice; the heifer does not (337ff.).

8. The animals are killed, the heifer easily, the bull with difficulty (341ff.).
9. The entrails are removed and examined (351ff.).
10. The slaughtered victims twitch (378ff.).

Other stage business occurs when Creo is dragged away to the dungeon (708f.) and when Iocasta seizes Oedipus' sword and commits suicide (1034).

Agamemno

A. *Entrance cues*. Entrance cues exist for Eurybates (408ff.), Cassandra with the secondary chorus (586ff.), Agamemno and Clytemnestra (775ff.), Strophius (913), Clytemnestra (947ff.), and Aegisthus (978). Characters who enter on entrance lines are the chorus (57), Aegisthus (226), and Electra with Orestes (910ff.). Silent entries are those of Clytemnestra at or slightly after 392a, and Cassandra at 867 if she has left the stage for the preceding choral ode.

B. *Exit cues*. Cued exits are those of Clytemnestra and Aegisthus into the palace at 308f., Agamemno to sacrifice at 802ff., Strophius with Orestes on the chariot at 941ff., Electra at 997ff., and Cassandra at 1001ff. Exits not textually cued are those of the Nutrix at 225, and Cassandra at 802ff. if she does not remain onstage for the following choral ode. But in view of Agamemno's order to the *famuli* to restrain Cassandra, it is probably likeliest that they take her into the palace and that she reenters after the ode.

The claim has been made[26] that the point at which the secondary chorus of Trojan captives exits is somehow problematic. To be sure, this is another uncued exit, but the most probable answer to the supposed problem is that this chorus remains onstage with Cassandra throughout Act III and exits with her and the *famuli* at 802ff.

C. *Identification cues*. Characters identified textually are the Umbra Thyestis (6), Clytemnestra (125), Aegisthus (233), Eurybates (408ff.), Cassandra (586ff.), the secondary chorus (586ff.), Agamemno (775ff.), Electra (910), Orestes (917), and Strophius and Pylades (918). The Nutrix is not textually identified and the problem of the identification of the primary chorus has already been discussed.[27]

D. *Stage business*. When the Umbra Thyestis addresses Aegisthus at 48ff. it is barely possible that Aegisthus is onstage in some sort of dumb-show, but this idea seems unnecessary. Other stage business involves Cassandra:

---

[26] Zwierlein, *ib.* 80-87.
[27] Above, p. 36.

1. She tears the fillet from her hair (693).
2. She goes into a mantic frenzy (710ff.).
3. She collapses. The chorus begins to help her but is interrupted by the triumphal entrance of Agamemno and Clytemnestra (775ff.).
4. After Clytemnestra exits Agamemno sees Cassandra and bids his *famuli* lift her up (787). Probably she momentarily escapes notice because she is lying on a different part of the stage.
5. Because of her bizarre responses to his questioning, Agamemno decides Cassandra is insane. He bids his *famuli* restrain her (800).
6. Probably they carry her off at the end of the act (and the secondary chorus exits here).

More stage business includes the arrival of Strophius on his chariot (918), Orestes mounting on the chariot and his disguise as an athletic victor, involving an onstage costume-change (935ff.), Electra going to the altar (951), and her forcible removal as the *famuli* drag her off (997ff.).

Thyestes

A. *Entrance cues.* The only entrance cue in the play is that for Thyestes at 908ff. Most other characters enter on entrance lines: the Furia (23), the chorus (122), Atreus (176), Thyestes with Tantalus (404), Atreus (491), the Nuntius (623), and Atreus with his *famuli* (885). The entrance of the Satelles at 176 is textually unmarked.

B. *Exit cues.* No exit is cued. Unmarked exits include those of the Umbra Tantali with the Furia (191), Atreus and the Satelles (335), Thyestes with his children and Atreus (545), and the Nuntius (788).

C. *Identification cues.* Characters identified in the text when they first appear are the Umbra Tantali (2f.), Atreus (180), Thyestes (404, 410), and Tantalus (421). Unidentified characters are the Furia, presumably identifiable by a distinctive mask,[28] the chorus, the Satelles, and the Nuntius.

D. *Stage business.* At 121 the Umbra Tantali and the Furia exit by passing into the palace. As suggested in an earlier context,[29] this might be deemed a visual metaphor. Some stage effect could possibly accompany Atreus' description of the trembling palace at 260ff.[30] At 517ff. Thyestes falls at Atreus' knees and at 521f. Atreus embraces him and his children. At 544f. Atreus puts a crown on Thyestes' head. After the banqueting Thyestes has been produced on the *exostra* at 908ff., Atreus gives him a cup (982f.) and then shows him the remains of his son (1004f.). At 1043 Thyestes tries to seize Atreus' sword.

---

[28] Cf. the Fury mask mentioned at Pollux, *Onomasticon* 4.142.

[29] Above, p. 24. Of course the use of such visual images as this and the recurrent sword in the *Phaedra* constitutes further evidence that Seneca was writing for the stage.

[30] Above, p. 24.

Hercules Oetaeus

A. *Entrance cues*. Cued entrances are those of Lichas (567f.), the main chorus (581f.), Deianira (700ff.), Hyllus (740f.), Hercules (1130), Alcmena (1337), Philoctetes (1693ff.), and Alcmena (1755ff.). Characters who enter on entrance lines are the secondary chorus (104), Iole (173), the Nutrix (233, 563), and Hyllus (1419). Textually unmarked entrances are those of the Nutrix when she enters with Deianira at 700ff. and Hyllus in Act V, who first speaks at 1831: most likely he enters with Alcmena at 1758.

B. *Exit cues*. Cued exits are those of the Nutrix at 538ff., Deianira at 1023f., Hyllus at 1029f., Hercules at 1512ff., and Alcmena at 1981f. Uncued exits are those of Hercules at 103, Iole and the secondary chorus at 232 (an exit cue or an entrance cue immediately thereafter would have helped indicate the change of setting between Acts I and II), Deianira, the Nutrix, and Lichas at 582, the Nutrix with Deianira and Hyllus at the end of Act III (i.e. at 1023ff.) if not earlier (she speaks her last line at 715), and Philoctetes at 1757 when he last speaks, or shortly thereafter, in order to free the protagonist for the role of Hercules.

C. *Identification cues*. The following characters are identified in the text: Hercules (6, also identified by his distinctive costume), the secondary chorus (119ff.), Iole (identified by description at 207ff., named at 278), Deianira (241, before she enters), Lichas (567f.), the primary chorus (581f.), Hyllus (740), Alcmena (1137), and Philoctetes (1603ff.). The only character not given an identification cue in the text is the Nutrix.

D. *Stage business*. In a play that is otherwise overlong and excessively verbose, the level of excitement is scarcely helped by a predominant absence of physical action. At 482f. Deianira and the Nutrix look around to make sure the coast is clear. At 1262f. Hercules tears off a bloody chunk of his flesh,[31] at 1402 he swoons, and at 1405f. extras remove his weapons. Towards the end of the play Alcmena produces an urn bearing the ashes of the incinerated hero (1759).

While we have uncovered no evidence that establishes that the *Hercules Oetaeus* was not written for stage production, the contrast between this play and the genuine Senecan tragedies goes a long way towards emphasizing the actual theatrical qualities of the latter.

Phoenissae

There are no definite entrance cues in this collection of dramatic scenes and only a couple of exit cues. When Oedipus says at lines 359ff.:

---

[31] For difficulties involved in this action cf. Zwierlein, *op. cit.* 27-29.

> *latebo rupis exesae cavo*
> *aut sepe densa corpus abstrusum tegam.*

this might indicate an exit into the stage building if the *scaenae frons* represents a cave. Otherwise Oedipus must conceal himself behind some other scenic feature. Another exit cue is that for Iocasta at 427 (cf. also 403 and 407). Other characters enter on entrance lines: Oedipus with Antigone guiding him at the beginning of the play, Iocaste with Antigone at 363, and the Satelles at 387. It is not clear that what we have at 443ff. is supposed to be the beginning of an act. If so, perhaps improbably 443ff. must be regarded as Iocasta's entry lines. Are Polynices and Eteocles already onstage or are they supposed to enter silently at this point?

It is a striking fact that no character in these scenes is ever identified by name, only by the specification of a relationship. Oedipus is Laius' son (40ff.), Antigone his daughter (2, 43), Iocasta her mother (403) and queen (387); of the sons, Polynices is identified as the one who has been exiled (466) and we are left to deduce Eteocles' identity by the process of elimination. The Satelles is wholly unidentified.

What little stage business exists is found in the final scene. Iocasta embraces Polynices (464) and bids him put off his shield and helmet (470ff.). He does so but turns away his head to keep a close eye on his brother (473f.). Then she allows him to rearm and tells Eteocles to disarm (480ff.). Eteocles complies (498f.).

As mentioned above,[32] the pervasive absence of implicit stage directions in these sketches prompts the suggestion that Seneca would have paid more attention to dramaturgy, resolved evident problems regarding such issues as the setting of the play, and added more passages of a stage direction nature, at a later stage of composition.

CONCLUSION

> There are of course three possibilities. Seneca wrote his tragedies for recitation, he wrote them for performance and they were performed, or he wrote them for performance and they were never performed in antiquity. For the critic the last two are the same.

Thus a recent writer on Seneca.[33] Broadly speaking, these are the choices before us although, as we shall see, the possibility that Seneca's plays were written for performance, actual or at least intended, bifurcates into two further choices.

---

[32] Above, pp. 15f.
[33] Calder, *op. cit.* (*1976*) 4.

Let it be confessed at the outset of this summary that nothing set forth in this study proves in anything approaching an absolute way which one of these possibilities is correct. Nevertheless the cumulative results are very suggestive.

All ancient dramatic texts have perforce, because of the absence of stage directions, certain information "encoded" in the words spoken by actors and the chorus: cues and other similar information that may collectively be designated implicit stage directions. Even a casual reading of Senecan tragedy reveals that such information is found in his texts no less than in those of any other ancient playwright. On the other hand, if his plays were (uniquely, among available ancient dramatic texts) meant for recitation rather than for actual dramatic performance, one might think that their texts would reveal special features, such as passages addressing the problem of character-identification that, as suggested in the Introduction, would be specific to recitation. No such features exist.

If Seneca's dramatic texts are loaded with features which look precisely like the implicit stage directions universally characteristic of ancient drama, the presence of such information is susceptible to two possible interpretations. Either they may be taken as positive evidence that Seneca was writing for the stage, or they must be explained according to the assumption that Seneca was only maintaining the fiction of writing for dramatic production.

It might seem a reasonable assumption that if Seneca were only including such passages in his plays as a matter of fiction, this would readily be demonstrable because he would presumably take no great pains to ensure that the 'implicit stage directions' inserted in his texts make good theatrical sense. Therefore, according to this line of reasoning, the best way to determine whether he was writing for stage production is to examine this kind of information closely: if it is consistent and makes sense, and if it suggests that Senecan drama could have been produced according to the dramatic conventions and with the theatrical resources of Seneca's day, then the proper conclusion would be that Seneca was writing for the stage; if it is inconsistent and nonsensical, then it may collectively be dismissed as fictitious and Seneca may be thought to have been writing for recitation only.

Such was the reasoning of Zwierlein (and of course of those whose arguments he inherited and assembled into a comprehensive study). We are indebted to Zwierlein and others who have transformed previous anti-staging arguments by making an objective and reasonably stated case founded on the close observation of the internal evidence of the plays. Yet in so doing, they have exposed the central flaws of their case, which in large measure is founded on two misconceptions. The first is the frequent tendency to mistake signs of ineptitude for probative evidence that Seneca's plays were not meant to, or could not, be produced on the stage. To be sure, signs of ineptitude are present. Yet what do they really tell us except that which is universally conceded in any event—that Seneca was a dilettante playwright? The claim that lapses from the standards of excellent dramaturgy established by the best of the Greeks go to show that Seneca was not writing for the stage reveals an egregious lack of proportion. The second weakness of the anti-stage case is a pervasive obliviousness to the artificial and often irrational conventions of the ancient theater. What is the point of berating Seneca for observing dramatic conventions also followed by other playwrights? When the allegations of the anti-stage party to the effect that Seneca's internal stage directions are nonsensical which run afoul of these two pitfalls are subtracted, and when various supposed problems are shown to be non-problematic, what remains? Surely not enough talking-points to sustain the argument that Seneca was not writing for the theater.

This is one thing revealed by this study. Another thing brought to light is the striving after genuine theatricality, visual and verbal alike, which bespeaks an interest in producing powerful effects on an audience. Modern readers may not respond, may in fact even disparage some of the means by which Seneca sought to achieve his effects. But let us confess that such a reaction betrays the taste of an age, especially of an age that regards rhetoric of the bombastic sort with profound mistrust. The Elizabethans of course felt very differently about Senecan drama[34] and responded eagerly to values towards which we are indifferent if not downright hostile.[35] We have no right to say that because Senecan tragedy does not correspond to our notion of what drama ought to be, it is therefore not drama at all.

But if we are to decide that Seneca was writing with dramatic production in mind, the choices confronting us are by no means exhausted. We must then face the additional problem that some authorities think these plays were written for some kind of closet performance in a domestic

---

[34] Besides T.S. Eliot, "Seneca in Elizabethan Translations," in his *Selected Essays* (New York, 1932) cf. F. Kiefer, "Seneca's Influence on Elizabethan Tragedy: An Annotated Bibliography," *Research Opportunities in Renaissance Drama* 21 (1978) 17-34.

[35] This prejudice is exhibited even by professional students of Elizabethan tragedy. Consider, for instance, the statement of John Bakeless, *The Tragicall History of Christopher Marlowe* (Cambridge, Mass, 1942) I.245, "[Marlowe's] other faults, bombast, rant, and bloodshed, were re-enforced by the influence of Seneca; and together they encouraged the welter of bloodshed in which Elizabethan playwrights delighted. This evil influence is felt almost to the closing of the theaters in 1642." Here ambiguous writing leaves one guessing what precisely is meant by "This evil influence": the influence of Seneca, of Marlowe, or of both?

household,[36] and this idea would appear to square with the interpretation of Senecan drama one sometimes encounters that these plays are written for the edification of *cognoscenti*, as dramatic illustrations of the Stoic philosophy, or possibly for the edification and instruction (or even as vehicles for the acting) of Nero; or again, some might argue for closet performance for a different reason—the harsh representation of autocracy in some of these plays would be too politically subversive for public performance in the reigns of Claudius or Nero.[37]

If we were to address this question in all its ramifications, we should be taken well beyond the bounds of the present study. We should have to consider such issues as the relation of Seneca's tragedies to the Stoic philosophy and to the politics of Seneca's times, which would in turn involve us in the question of when these plays were written. However we can make a reasonable start towards answering it on the basis of observations made in the course of this investigation.

In the first place, if Seneca's tragedies were written for dramatic production at all, there is little room for doubt that they were written for production in a full-scale theater. We have seen that the plays variously presuppose the availability of most if not all of the stage machinery of the theater. We have seen that they presume the availability of actors, mutes, extras (a rather large number in one case),[38] and children, and also of two choruses simultaneously on the stage. We have also seen indications of a large *pulpitum*. In the *Agamemno* the protagonist enters and at first fails to see the prostrate Cassandra. In the *Phaedra* Theseus finds it necessary to order the dead Hippolytus to be brought to his part of the stage. And in the same play Hippolytus asks (430f.):

> quid huc seniles fessa moliris gradus,
> o fida nutrix(?)

The Nutrix has already been on the stage, so rather than marking her entry these lines must indicate that at this point she crosses the stage. In

---

[36] This is the view of Calder in the articles cited in this study. At *op. cit.* (*1976*) he argues the case most fully and comes to the conclusion that "Senecan tragedy, like Propertian elegy, was in the nature of côterie poetry." Calder notices the evidence for domestic performance of drama under the early Empire at *ib.* 132 with n.1 and concludes that domestic performances would be small-scale affairs using portable stages, choruses of reduced size, etc. He especially points to Plutarch, *Crassus* 33, which describes how after a banquet the furniture was cleared away for a performance of Euripides' *Bacchae*.

[37] This is one of Calder's arguments (cf. n. 41 below). If true, this would exclude the argument that Seneca wrote these tragedies for Nero's education and edification, or as vehicles for his acting. So, e.g., Gilbert Highet, *The Classical Tradition* (Oxford, 1949) 598 n.10 (he evidently never fulfilled his promise of writing an article on the subject), who thought of Nero's *domestica scaena* mentioned by Tacitus, *Annales* 15.39.

[38] Above, p. 34.

several plays a character is able to speak on his part of the stage without fear of being overheard.[39] The *Medea* requires the two-building "set." Furthermore, according to Vitruvius 5.6.2 and 5.7.2 the chorus as well as the actors (which is essentially what he means by the *thymelici* and the *scaenici*) stood on the stage in contrast to the Greek practice of locating the chorus in the *orchestra* where it could dance. So Seneca's choruses and extras shared space on the *pulpitum*. All these considerations suggest a large theater.

In the second place, we have seen signs of Seneca catering to what seems identifiable as popular taste (and in the following Appendix further evidence for this will be presented). In Senecan tragedy, one might care to allege, the graphic delving into physical horror and the supernatural, and also the catering to enthusiasm for performing animals, might so be characterized.[40]

Those who argue for private domestic performance run the risk of adopting a false position. The present study was begun with a dichotomous proposition: the passages in Senecan tragedy that appear to be implicit stage directions *either* actually refer to the author's intentions for the production of these plays *or* are inserted because the poet was maintaining the fiction that such was his purpose. But since the passages in question point to the conclusion that Seneca had in mind production in a large, well-equipped theater, those who argue for small-scale domestic performance seem to be reduced to the contention that the implicit stage directions suggesting production in a large theater are fictitious *but nevertheless* Seneca was writing for that form of production. This would be a peculiar argument.

So the weight of the evidence indicates that Seneca intended his plays for production in a normal Roman theater. Obviously this discovery has profound implications for the way in which we should and should not read and interpret these plays. Equally obviously, a number of questions are raised. To the best of our knowledge, the only theaters large and well-equipped enough to permit the staging of Seneca's tragedies were the public ones. Then, are we to think that Seneca was writing for the general public, despite the fact that some of his plays contain material that looks politically subversive?[41] Or should we think that the facilities

---

[39] Above, p. 39.

[40] Of course the rebuttal is always available that the tastes of an elite can become tainted by popular taste. However I prefer to stand by this characterization, guided by Cicero. His aversion to the taste of the theatergoing *vulgus* is instructive. Cf. such passages as *Tusculan Disputations* 1.37 (with special reference to the supernatural), *ad Familiares* 7.1.2 (with special reference to stage spectacle, including the use of animals on the stage), *pro Murena* 40, and *de Officiis* 2.60.

[41] This is most true of the *Thyestes*: cf. Calder, *op. cit. (1983)*.

available for private performance (in Nero's *domestica scaena*, if nowhere else), were sufficiently elaborate to meet the demands of Senecan tragedy? In any event, any speculation about why, when, or for whom these plays were written must be balanced against the internal evidence which distinctly tends to show that they were intended for a large, well-appointed theater.

There is, in sum, no evidence that any Senecan play was actually produced in antiquity.[42] But there is an equal absence of convincing internal evidence that their author did not write them with the expectation, or at least the hope, that they would be brought to the stage. Quite to the contrary, we have uncovered a number of reasons for thinking that he gave considerable, if not always equally successful, thought to their staging. There is no reason for denying Seneca the title of playwright in the full sense of the word.

---

[42] This fact has also been alleged as an argument that Seneca was writing for domestic performance only: the argument does not take into account the possibility that Seneca was writing for public performance but that his plays were never produced in antiquity. Note too that at least one Senecan tragedy was sufficiently well known that a line from it could turn up as a Pompeian graffito (*Ag.* 730 = *CIL* iv 2.6698 in the form IDAI CERNU NEMURA). And for paintings possibly inspired by Senecan plays cf. M. Bieber, *The History of the Greek and Roman Theater* (Princeton, 1961) 229-234.

ARTIFICIAL BLOOD IN THE ROMAN THEATER

Four Senecan tragedies feature onstage bloodshed. In the *Hercules Furens* the protagonist kills one of his sons in sight of the audience, as Medea kills both of her children in the *Medea*. In the *Phaedra* and the *Oedipus* Phaedra and Iocasta kill themselves with swords. In addition, in the *Medea* the heroine gashes her arm and her blood pours on the altar, and the *Oedipus* features the onstage sacrifice of two cattle. Since with the sole exception of Ajax' onstage suicide in Sophocles' *Ajax* such scenes of onstage bloodshed cannot be matched in Greek drama, it is generally understood that there was some kind of injunction, maybe religious in nature, against the representation of onstage bloodshed on the Greek stage.[1] Therefore, not unnaturally, the fact that Seneca's tragedies repeatedly feature onstage bloodshed has been held up as further reason for doubting that the poet was writing for stage production.[2]

So it is worth pointing out that unambiguous evidence does exist for onstage bloodshed in the Roman theater of the first century A.D. The evidence is preserved in connection with a pair of plays produced in the presence of Caligula the day before his assassination. Suetonius, *Caligula* 57, writes:

Sacrificans respersus est phoenicopteri sanguine. et pantomimus Mnester tragoediam saltavit, quam olim Neoptolemus tragoedius ludis, quibus rex Macedonum Philippus occisus est, egerat; et cum in Laureolo mimo, in quo actor proripiens se ruina sanguinem vomit, plures secundarum certatim experimentum artis darent, cruore scaena abundavit.

Further details are provided by Josephus, *Jewish Antiquities* 19, 94:

ἔνθα δὲ καὶ σημεῖα δυὸ γενέσθαι· καὶ γὰρ μῖμος εἰσάγεται, καθ᾽ ὃν σταυροῦται ληφθεὶς (λῃστὴς Bulengerus, λῃστῶν Hudson) ἡγεμών, ὅ τε ὀρχηστὴς δρᾶμα εἰσάγει Κινύραν, ἐν ᾧ αὐτός τε ἐκτείνετο καὶ ἡ θυγάτηρ Μύρρα, αἷμα τε ἦν τεχνητὸν πολὺ καὶ τὸ περὶ τὸν σταυρωθέντα ἐκκεχυμένον καὶ τὸ περὶ τὸν Κινύραν.

Josephus adds that the performance in question fell on the same day of the year as Philip's murder.

Unfortunately, there is little to be said about the *Cinyras*. Since the *Cinyras* performed before Philip was an acted play and the present piece was danced by the tragic pantomime Mnester, it is doubtful that they

---

[1] Flickinger, *op. cit.* 130-132.
[2] Zwierlein, *op. cit.* 24-29.

were one and the same play:[3] probably by *tragoediam saltavit, quam olim Neoptolemus...egerat* Suetonius means to intimate no more than that they were works on the same mythological subject. For the myth of Cinyras and Myrrha, whose incestuous relationship led to the birth of Adonis, one may consult the references provided by Sir James Frazer at vol. II, p. 84 n.1 of the Loeb Library edition of Ps.-Apollodorus' *Library*. The myth was given Roman currency by Ovid in Book X of the *Metamorphoses* (cf. also, e.g., Hyginus, *Fabula* 58) but the play attested by Josephus can scarcely have followed the Ovidian account which features no deaths.

We are better informed regarding the *Laureolus* mime, as other references exist. The first is Juvenal 8.185ff. (upon which the Scholiast adds nothing of interest):

> consumptis opibus vocem, Damasippe, locasti
> sipario, clamosum ageres ut Phasma Catulli.
> Laureolum velox etiam bene Lentulus egit,
> iudice me dignus vera cruce.

A second reference to the *Laureolus* may exist in Juvenal. At 13.111 some think that *fugitivus scurra Catulli* (upon which the Scholiast comments *talia est enim mimus, ubi fugitivus dominum suum trahit*) refers to the *Laureolus*. Others demur.[4]

Tertullian, *in Valent*. 14, adds a passing reference. The Gnostic Achamoth is unable to surmount the cross of Matter (*supervolare crucem*) because she had not yet learned to play the part in Catullus' *Laureolus*.

Finally, Martial attests to a perverse performance of the mime in the time of Domitian (*de Spectac*. 7: a second such ghastly performance may be attested at Martial 10.25):

> qualiter in Scythica religatus rupe Prometheus
> adsiduam nimio pectore pavit avem,
> nuda Caledonio sic viscera praebuit urso
> non falsa pendens in cruce Laureolus.
> vivebant laceri membris stillantibus artus
> inque omni nusquam corpore corpus erat.
> denique supplicium.............................
> vel domini iugulum foderat ensa nocens,
> templa vel arcano demens spoliaverat auro,
> subdiderat saevas vel tibi, Roma, faces.
> viverat antiquae sceleratus crimina famae,
> in quo, quae fuerat fabula, poena fuit.

Since literary historians often write of Roman mime, or at least mime of the Empire in contrast to that of the Republic when writers such as

---

[3] *Pace* Kannicht-Snell, *TrGF* 2.11.5a.

[4] Cf. the *RE* article "Laureolus" [Lieben]; the reference at Juvenal 13.11 does not concern the *Laureolus* mime according to Ribbeck, *CRF* 371.

Decimus Laberius and Pubilius Syrus flourished, as a subliterary theatrical form, it is interesting and important to observe that Catullus' *Laureolus* and *Phasma*[5] were plays written by an author who clearly enjoyed a certain vogue. According to Cicero,[6] the mime was already replacing Atellan farce as the *exodium* or comic afterpiece to more serious dramatic productions in his day. Here we have rare, maybe even unique, evidence for an actual instance of double billing where the titles and contents of the pieces performed are preserved.

One naturally wants to know that Suetonius means by *plures secundarum certatim experimentum artis darent*. In his Loeb edition of Suetonius J.C. Rolphe confidently asserts "the actors *secundarum partium* entertained the spectators after a play by imitating the actions of the star." It is difficult to sustain this view in the light of Horace, *Ep.* 1.18.12ff.:

> *sic iterat voces et verba cadentia tollit,*
> *ut puerum saevo credas dictata magistro*
> *reddere vel partis mimum tractare secundas.*

On the showing of this passage it seems likelier that the actors *secundarum partium* aped the actions of the *archimimus* more or less simultaneously, perhaps behind his back.

It is not easy to assemble a coherent picture of the contents of the *Laureolus* mime from the scattered notices reproduced here. Some think of it as the story of a robber-chieftain,[7] perhaps originally a runaway slave if Laureolus is indeed Juvenal's *fugitivus scurra Catulli*, evidently captured and crucified. In view of Tertullian's allusion to Achamoth failing to escape the cross, however,[8] John Ferguson, a recent commentator on Juvenal, seems closer to the mark in suggesting:[9]

> Apparently the robber was caught and crucified, escaped somehow from the cross, but died of his wounds. This is the only way to reconcile the accounts.

It may not be irrelevant to cite Cicero, *pro Caelio* 22.66:

---

[5] If the *Laureolus* prefigured Senecan interest in gore, the *Phasma* may well have anticipated the poet's fascination with the supernatural.

[6] *Ad fam.* 9.17.1. Cicero however was premature in pronouncing the demise of the Atellana. We even hear of Atellanae performed in the time of Hadrian (Aelianus Spartianus, *Hadrian* 26.4).

[7] The reading ληφθείς ἡγεμών need not be questioned to support this view insofar as ἡγεμών itself can mean "robber chieftain" according to K.H. Rengstorf, *A Complete Concordance to Flavius Josephus* (Leiden, 1975) II.283.iii. Or could Laureolus have led a band of pirates?

[8] To be sure, one finds no lexicon definition of *supervolare* that supports this interpretation. Cf. however the Rev. A. Roberts and James Donaldson, *The Ante-Nicene Fathers* (New York, 1899-1900, repr. Grand Rapids, 1963) III. 511 n.11.

[9] John Ferguson, *Juvenal: The Satires* (New York, 1979) 241f.

mimi ergo est iam exitus, non fabulae; in quo cum clausula non invenitur,
fugit aliquis e manibus, deinde scabilla concrepant, aulaeum tollitur.

Evidently it was common to bring mimes to abrupt endings by staging implausible rescues and escapes.

The affinities of mime and romance are well known. The Greek romances display an abiding interest in robbers, and the *Scheintod* is a stock theme in that genre. In the present context one thinks specifically of Xenophon, *Ephesiaca* 4.2, where Habrocomes is lashed to a cross but then the cross is blown over by a high wind and the hero is rescued (there is another aborted crucifixion at Chariton 4.2.6 and the *Scheintod* also figures at, e.g., Heliodorus 8.9ff.). So it is scarcely improbable that the *Laureolus* mime may have featured this narrative device. However the suggestion that the robber died of his wounds is not supported by the evidence. Possibly he died in some other way, or even escaped entirely. The *Laureolus* mime may have been a kind of Roman *Beggars' Opera* that dramatized the career of a fictitious or even a real rogue. After all, from the romances it is clear that robbers and pirates were regarded as romantic and colorful fellows in antiquity no less than in eighteenth century England, and comedy perennially tolerates or glamorizes rogues and rascals.

In several ways the *Laureolus* mime looks like a valuable index to the tastes of an age. In the first place, it is difficult to consider Greek and Roman mimes without being impressed by resemblances with Greek romance and Roman novel. Three kinds of resemblance are striking. First, both novel and mime were governed by an enthusiasm for "realism"; the guiding ethos of the *biologoi* is equally visible in both genres.[10] Second, while we can scarcely specify with precision the audience for which ancient novels, particularly the Greek romances, were written, it is at least likely that such literature, like mimes, were popular fare. Third, a number of the same dramatic situations and narrative elements can be found in both genres. With respect to the so-called *Chariton* mime from Oxyrhynchus, this fact has been admirably discussed by Trenker.[11] The same point could be made about the class of Graeco-Roman mimes that has been discussed under the generic title of "The Adultery Mime,"[12] since adultery is a prominent theme in romance.[13]

---

[10] This point has been made by H. Reich, *Der Mimus* (Berlin, 1903, repr. Hildesheim, 1974) 35.

[11] Sophie Trenker, *The Greek Novella in the Classical Period* (Cambridge U.K., 1958) 53-55.

[12] R.W. Reynolds, "The Adultery Mime," *CQ* 40 (1946) 77-84.

[13] Trenker, *op. cit.* 189 index s.v. "love, adulterous."

What we have observed about the *Laureolus* mime is further evidence in support of the same conclusion.

Then too, the *Laureolus* mime caters to a taste for sensationalism. It is not entirely trivial to note that the testimonia pertaining to the dramatic performances the day before the death of Caligula constitute our earliest evidence for the use of artificial blood on the stage. Until now there had been no need to develop a technology of blood-bags or whatever devices were employed to squirt artificial blood for the audience's delectation, catering at once to cravings for realism and sensationalism.[14]

There is probably no coincidence that, not very long after this notorious set of performances, Seneca should have written tragedies featuring onstage violence and bloodshed, nor is it improbable that Seneca's plays contemplate the use of the same techniques for the use of artificial blood attested in connection with the *Cinyras* and the *Laureolus*. Like these plays, Senecan tragedy seems geared to cater to this same appetite for sensation. And one is of course tempted to think that this craving is not wholly unrelated to what transpired in the amphitheater.[15] Both verbally and visually Seneca is catering to this appetite to a degree unprecedented, as far as we know, in ancient tragedy. And if the sensationalism of Senecan tragedy seems calculated to appeal to contemporary popular taste, here too we have a significant indication that he was writing for performance in a public theater and scarcely for some kind of intellectual côterie.

---

[14] My Irvine colleague B. P. Reardon points out to me that such a technology is attested by Achilles Tatius. At 3.15 a girl is apparently disembowelled. But at 3.20 we learn that this was just a sham, achieved by a Homer-performer's trick knife (with a retractable blade) and a pouch full of sheep guts.

[15] The idea that theater audiences' tastes had been affected by the spectacles is scarcely a new one: cf. Herrmann, *op. cit.* (*1924*) 230, T. Siemers, *Seneca's Hercules Furens en Euripides' Heracles* (diss. Utrecht, 1951) 50, Bieber, *op. cit.* 105 and N. Tadic-Gilloteaux at *AC* 1963, 550.

USE OF THE TWO-BUILDING "SET"
IN THE *MEDEA*

It has been shown that the *Medea* uniquely requires a two-building "set." Both the royal palace of Corinth and Medea's house are visible to the audience and both buildings provide doors by which actors may enter and leave the stage. How precisely is this special "set" to be used? Fortunately, the comings and goings of the actors are indicated textually with sufficient clarity that this question can be addressed. The guiding principle is naturally that Medea and members of her household (the Nutrix, the children, possibly a paedagogue) enter and exit from Medea's house, while Creo, Iason, their various servants and followers, and the Nuntius enter and exit from the palace.

We have no idea of the actual dimensions of the "set" for which Seneca wrote (if we assume that he wrote with any particular theater in mind). But surely dramatic space, like dramatic time, is more flexible than its real-life counterpart and so, no matter what the actual size of the Senecan theater, the audience is required to assume that these buildings are sufficiently close that a person standing before one of them can see someone standing before the other (445f.) or even hear the creak of the other building's opening door (177f.). Nevertheless these structures are to be understood as sufficiently separated so that a character standing before one of them can speak a monologue not overheard by the other (179ff., 431ff.). An audience familiar with the scenic conventions of Roman comedy would accept such conventions automatically. Or, more precisely, there are a number of Roman scenic conventions that are illustrated by the plays of Plautus and Terence but undocumented in the relatively scanty evidence for pre-Senecan tragedy. How much Seneca is innovating by appropriating the scenic conventions of comedy regarding stage setting as well as in other respects noted at various points in this study, or how much these conventions were common to both Roman comedy and tragedy, is a question that cannot be settled on the basis of our evidence.

The probable movements of the actors on this unique two-building "set" may now be described. At the beginning of Act I Medea enters from her house and speaks the prologue (the Nutrix enters at least by line 116, but is perhaps with her all along). From 116f. it is clear that Medea has heard the chorus' parodos, and so in all probability she does not exit during this part of the play; it is likely that the chorus sings this marriage-hymn clustered around the palace. Meanwhile Medea, standing before her house, overhears it. In Act II, after the two women play out a standard Senecan domina-nutrix scene, Creo enters from the palace. At 186 Medea crosses the stage to speak with him (the Nutrix may or may not retire from the scene here), and at the end of this interview Medea and Creo return to their respective buildings.

At the beginning of Act III (380) Medea bursts out of her house, probably pursued by a frantic Nutrix. At 431 Iason enters from the palace, and by 445f. Medea sees him. 444 shows that he crosses to her side of the stage for their dialogue. The symmetrical staging of the Medea-Creo and Medea-Iason interviews looks deliberate. At 559 Iason exits, leaving Medea and the Nutrix before the house. This is the place where the sacrificial scene of Act IV is enacted. As noted in the text of this study, the fact that this event occurs on Medea's side of the stage mitigates the objection that such a transaction ought not to occur in broad daylight, thereby risking placing Medea's intended victims on their guard.

At the end of Act IV the children, under the tutelage either of the Nutrix or a hypothetical paedagogue, enter from Medea's house. Receiving the tainted gifts, they cross over the stage and exit into the palace. Then at the beginning of Act V the Nuntius bursts out of the palace to announce the catastrophe within. Medea and the Nutrix overhear him from their part of the stage (once it is realized that the play uses the two-building "set," the problem discussed by Costa[1] in his note on line 879 disappears). Medea's killing of the children occurs in front of and atop her house, with Iason and his retinue entering from the palace. Again, there is deliberate symmetry in the burning of the one building at the beginning of Act V and the burning of the other at the end.

A difficulty is brought to light by this analysis. This involves the movement of the children at the end of Act IV. In Euripides, Medea sends the gift-bearing children to Creon's daughter (969ff.); then (1002ff.) they return to her escorted by the paedagogue, so that they are present to be killed by their mother. But in Seneca, they are sent over to the palace. Next they appear when Medea addresses them at 945ff. But their return from the palace to Medea's house is not textually mentioned.

Three explanations may be offered. The first is simply that this is an oversight on the part of the author. Especially if they are supposed to be accompanied by some such extra as the paedagogue rather than the Nutrix, a speaking character, Seneca may have lost track of these mute

---

[1] C.D.N. Costa, *Seneca's Medea* (Oxford, 1973).

children. Another explanation is that the return of the children and their adult escort is represented in dumb-show during the chorus beginning at line 849. We have seen that it is likely that a funeral cortege occurs in dumb-show during the final chorus of the *Phaedra*.

The third possibility involves line 891f.:

> *effer citatum sede Pelopea gradum,*
> *Medea, praeceps quaslibet terras pete.*

The manuscripts are divided in giving these lines to the Nuntius or the Nutrix. In his commentary on these lines Costa argues in favor of the Nutrix, although he observes that in Euripides it is the Messenger who gives similar advice (1121ff.). But suppose that the speaker is the Nutrix. How, it would then deserve to be asked, does she know that a catastrophe has occurred and that her mistress ought to flee? A possible solution to this question, and to the problem at hand, might be found in the supposition that the Nutrix has escorted the children into the palace at the end of Act IV. Now she speaks these two lines as she emerges from the palace, accompanied by the two children. Then, more or less as she speaks, the three cross back to Medea's side of the stage and the children are delivered to their mother's not-so-tender mercies in response to her summons at 945f.

INDEX LOCORUM

(references to *loci* in Classical works are in italics: page-numbers of this book are printed in Roman type)

I. Seneca's Tragedies and the *Hercules Oetaeus*

II. OTHER AUTHORS

Printed in the United States
By Bookmasters